Mick Webber

Garaging London's Red Buses

Capital Transport

Cover: A busy scene inside Chelverton Road Putney garage in the mid-1930s. Eleven members of staff are in view cleaning buses, one suspects for the camera, and performing various checks. The four STLs nearest the camera are 1457, 1324, 1331 and 1327, with STL 1326 being the sixth one in the line.

Back Cover: A large proportion of Upton Park's allocation of buses are at home here on 12th March 1967. RTs are in abundance, with RML2598 and a sister vehicle on the right. (Mick Webber)

Above: Uxbridge garage in September 1936. This garage consisted of a single shed until another was added in 1955. Vehicles here are T 4, DA 6, DA 13 and ST 765. All of these had bodywork built by the LGOC. (LTM)

Title: In the early years of London Transport, the General fleet name was still used, and this is the case with this Dennis Lance seen parked at the front of Potters Bar garage in the early years of the Board. (Richard Stevenson Collection)

INTRODUCTION

When the London Passenger Transport Board came into being in July 1933, it inherited, and used, fifty two central area bus garages, and thirty five tram depots. Most of the north river tram depots were later converted to trolleybus operation between 1935 and 1940, and the remainder became bus garages after the abandonment of tramway operations between 1950 and 1952. When the trolleybus network was abandoned starting in 1959 and concluding in 1962, most of these depots also became bus garages. After economy measures, and early closures, the total of central bus garages was at its maximum in 1962, and stood at seventy one. The garages are dealt with during the fifty years from takeover by London Transport in July 1933 to June 1983, with a brief history, interior and exterior photographs and a location map. In 1984 London Transport was replaced by London Regional Transport as a first step to the introduction of a new generation of independent operators on London's bus services.

Most readers of this book will be familiar with the systems of garage coding. Briefly, the earliest garages were simply lettered A, B, C etc, followed by AB, AC, AD etc. Tilling garages were given the codes TB, TC and TL (L for Lewisham). Later garages were give codes that bore some reference to the garage name: e.g. BK for Barking. Where garages were later renamed (e.g. the original Hanwell became Southall) the code was unchanged. A surprising number of the old pre-war garages still exist, with modifications and extensions to cater for bigger buses, and modern maintenance facilities. The opposite of this is the number of open sites now used to house buses without the traditional staff comforts.

My thanks go to the people who have helped me with this task, Laurie Akehurst, Peter Horner, Jim Hawkins, Robin Newell and Jim Whiting, and to the photographers whose work appears here. Thanks are also due to the London Transport Museum staff at Acton, who allowed me to go through their photographic archive. London Transport Museum/TfL photographs in this book are credited LTM.

Mick Webber

First published 2019

ISBN 978 1 85414 436 2

Published by Capital Transport Publishing Ltd
www.capitaltransport.com

Printed by Parksons Graphics

ABBEY WOOD (AW)

The London County Council built a new tramcar shed at Abbey Wood in 1910, and extended it in 1914. The London Passenger Transport Board took over operations in July 1933, and trams operated from here until conversion to buses on 6th July 1952. If the pre-war plans of converting trams to trolleybuses had been fulfilled, this would have been converted to trolleybuses, but the Second World War intervened, and after the cessation of hostilities in 1945, ideas had changed, and the remaining trams were replaced by motor buses. The depot was completely rebuilt to accommodate buses, although it was not completely ready when the trams finished, and some buses were operated from nearby Saunders Yard in Southland Road until the work was complete in September. RTLs were initially used being replaced by RTs in 1955, with RMs appearing in 1968 and subsequently more modern types, including the DMS and MD. With the ever expanding estate at Thamesmead needing more services, it was not possible to enlarge the garage, and along with nearby Plumstead (AM), it closed to traffic on 30th October 1981, with operations transferred to the new garage at Plumstead (PD) the following day. Maximum vehicle requirement at closure was 36 and routes operated were 161, 177, 178, 180 and 272.

It is 4th February 1967, and RT 4334 is at home waiting to turn out on route 180 to Lower Sydenham. The building on the left housed offices on the ground floor, with a canteen on the first floor. The small road between this building and the garage was used for terminating buses on route 177. (Mick Webber)

The inspection pit area at Abbey Wood. The garage entrance is to the right, with the exit to the left. This June 1953 view shows RTLs 11, 1389 and 25. The RTL allocation was replaced by RTs in 1955. (LTM)

The first new garage built by London Transport was Alperton. It opened to traffic on 7th June 1939 with an STL allocation. The garage was involved in body overhauls during the war years, and many new 2RT2s were stored here in 1940, when their braking problems were being rectified. The garage also operated utility Guys, and in 1949 new RTWs were delivered here at a time when 8 feet wide buses were not permitted to operate in Central London. This allocation was short lived, when in 1950 RTLs and in 1951, RTs appeared. Routemasters were allocated in 1964. Single deckers from the MB and SMS classes began to emerge in 1969 and 1971, and the DMS in 1972. The garage was enlarged in 1978, when the adjacent building, previously occupied by the LT Lifts and escalators department, was incorporated into the main garage. The Metrobus became the main allocation in 1980, and the garage is still in operation today. Routes operated at April 1983 were 18, 79, 79A, 83, 182 and 187.

The Ealing Road door at Alperton on 25th February 1967. The LGOC style "Caution buses turning" sign and post can be seen on the left. (Mick Webber)

May 1950, and an interesting selection of buses are resting inside Alperton garage. From left to right are STL 617, G 45, STL 864, STL 1529, and G 98. At the end against the far wall, is RTW 74, with a "not to be started" sign on the cab door. This bus had been delivered new here in September 1949, and was about to be transferred to Chalk Farm. A member of the garage staff is attending to adverts on an STL on the right. (LTM)

ASH GROVE (AG)

The new garage at Ash Grove in Hackney was opened in 1981, and it replaced the old premises at Dalston and Hackney. It has since had an unfortunate career. Staff disputes and refusal to work new tenders resulted in the closure of the garage in November 1991. It reopened in May 1994, being used by Kentish Bus, but closed again in February 1998. It was used for a period to store some of the LT Museum fleet, until the store at Acton was ready to accommodate them. The garage opened again in March 2000 with East Thames Buses, an LT subsidiary, occupying the site. The routes operated at April 1983 were 6, 9, 11, 35, 106, 253, 502 and 513.

Below: The new garage at Ash Grove in April 1981. The builders sign is still in place, and finishing touches are being applied before service commences. The high walls and semi-circular towers make it look more like a prison than a bus garage perhaps. (Capital Transport)

Right: RM 793 leaves the garage at Ash Grove on 20th July 1981 to take up service on route 47. The run in blinds show "Cambridge Heath, Ash Grove garage". (LTM)

Below right: RM 2125 and RML 2566 can be seen in this view at Ash Grove on 13th June 1981. The RML is leaving, and the RM shows the adverts for the GLC scheme of 25p "Fare deal". (Peter Horner)

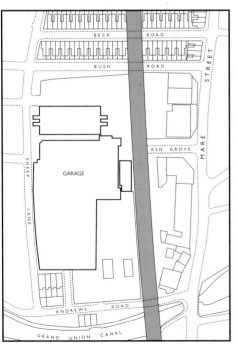

ATHOL STREET (C)

The roots of this garage go back a long way. It had been a horse bus depot from 1879. The London General Omnibus Company opened it as a bus garage on 1st July 1907. It has always been associated with the operation of the services through the Thames tunnels at Rotherhithe and Blackwall, where specially designed NS class buses with tapered sides and back to back upper deck seats were used. These were replaced with modified STL vehicles in 1937. The garage suffered many bombing incidents during the war, no doubt due to its close proximity to the docks. It also operated the special Port of London Authority route, which worked from Custom House to Manor Way Station, and was shared with Bow (BW) in the final year of operation. Its fate was sealed when nearby Poplar (PR) trolleybus depot was converted to buses in November 1959, as PR had an excess of space for the routes that were operated. The closure of Athol Street was delayed however, as it was used for meal relief for crews from routes on nearby East India Dock Road. This was resolved when a new canteen was opened, and Athol Street was closed on 9th May 1961, its fleet of RTLs being transferred to Poplar. Total maximum requirement for 1960 was 52. Routes operated at time of closure were 40, 56, 82, 108, 108A and the PLA route. After the war and with increasing road traffic, Athol Street was responsible for keeping Blackwall and Rotherhithe tunnels clear of all breakdowns. Breakdown lorry with crane 747P was allocated to Athol Street on 17th February 1949 until transferred to Poplar garage on 9th May 1961.

The area around the garage at Athol Street was devastated during the war, and not much had been done to rebuild the surrounding area when this picture was taken on 17th October 1959. The scars from previously adjoining buildings can clearly be seen. (John Gillham)

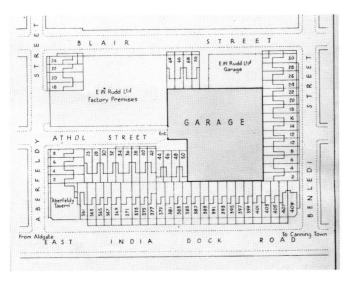

Athol Street was indeed a very dark place. The few skylight windows shed some light in this view taken on 7th January 1937, where STL 400 stands next to NS 2220. The tunnel NS is in its final year of service, and the class will soon be replaced by new STLs on tunnel routes 82 and 108. (LTM)

BARKING (BK)

The LGOC built their new garage at Barking, and opened it on 9th January 1924. The London County Council's new housing estates in the area warranted new routes and more buses, and Barking was at the forefront. It was enlarged in 1928. In the London Transport era, it operated a fleet of LTs, and later many utility Guys, which were eventually replaced by RTLs in 1949. RTs then took over in 1958, with a few RTWs for a short period. RMs were allocated from 1964, but numbers were few, and the DMS class started to appear in 1972, along with the one man single deckers. Barking will always be associated with running the last RT in Central service, when RT624 arrived home on route 62 on 7th April 1979. A proposed closure in 1992 did not occur, and the garage still functions today. Routes operated at April 1983 were 62, 87, 145, 148, 162, 169, 179, 238, 287 and N95.

The garage aspect on the corner of Longbridge Road, and South Park Drive. The LGOC initials in the stonework above the door can be seen in this pre-war view. The single storey building on the right, bears the name of its successor. A large parking area was provided on the far right. (LTM)

RTL 521 was at Barking between May 1951 and March 1954. During this period, it is seen blinded up for an excursion to Whipsnade Zoo, with a line-up of two RTLs and two Guys in the background. (D.A.Jones)

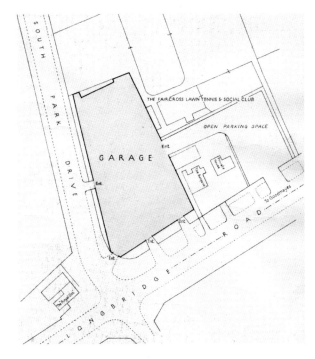

Barking famously operated the very last regular RT route and many people gathered at the garage on the last day, 7th April 1979, to see RT 624 arrive at the end of its final journey in London Transport service. The bus went on to see further service for a time with London Country. (Capital Transport)

BATTERSEA (B)

The London Road Car Company opened a bus garage in Hester Road, Battersea, on 1st July 1907, and it passed to the LGOC in 1908. The company opened an annexe on the south side of the road in 1914. In the mid-1930s a mix of STL and NS class buses were operated. The garage worked special Festival of Britain buses in 1951, and RT family vehicles arrived with RTLs and RTWs staying until 1967 and 1965 respectively. RTWs here were used in experiments in May, June and July 1950 to operate routes 19, 22 and 31 to prove to the police that it was safe to use 8 feet wide vehicles on routes in central London, where they had previously been banned. Routemasters were used from here in 1967, and eventually DMSs in 1972. The garage closed on 1st November 1985, but re-opened for the Sightseeing tours operations until April 1988. Stockwell used the annexe building as an outstation from June 1993 until June 1998. Many internal alterations and modifications were carried out during the 1960s, and in 1970, to try to bring the old building up to modern standards, but in the end work was transferred to the more modern establishments at Victoria and Wandsworth. Routes operated at April 1983 were 19, 22 and 39.

Battersea garage shows its age in this view on 7th May 1954. The permanently displayed advert for drivers and conductors shows just how bad the labour situation was at this time. The old layout and restricted access would prove to be a real problem in the future, as longer and wider vehicles became available. The annexe building is just out of view on the right. (LTM)

A light and airy Battersea is depicted here on 25th September 1936. Four NS class buses are in view, the first three, from left to right, are NS 800, 954 and 1654. Staff are attending to NS 954. The four show the NS in its final form with pneumatic tyres and top deck roofs. The NSs had been the first double deck buses to operate in London with a top deck roof and pneumatic tyres. (LTM)

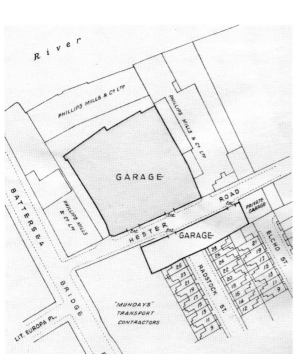

It is 1982, and this shot inside Battersea shows M 857, one of the new Metrobuses to arrive here. Alongside, are RMs 2162 and 325 blinded up for the 19. RM 325 was to spend 8 years here.

BEXLEYHEATH (BX)

Bexleyheath was the only completely new depot built for trolleybuses. Other trolleybus depots had been rebuilt or modernised existing tram depots, but the sites in the Bexley area were deemed unsuitable for the new form of transport. It was opened on 10th November 1935, and suffered two devastating bombings during the war. When trolleybuses were replaced on 4th March 1959, a fleet of RTs moved in, and were the only class allocated here until 1969. One man SM class buses came in 1970 for a short time, and DMSs in 1971. RTs finally bowed out in April 1978, when they were withdrawn from route 89. There is a substantial forecourt here used by terminating buses, and a large yard at the back, often used for storing withdrawn vehicles. The garage closed in August 1986, but reopened as a base for Bexleybus in January 1988. Routes operated at April 1983 were 89, 96, 99, 122A, 132 and 269. The garage still operates today.

RT 3911 is parked inside Bexleyheath garage in July 1972. It displays blinds for route 89, which was to be the last RT route operated here in 1978. This bus was delicensed in 1974, and transferred to Catford. It also saw service at New Cross, Highgate, Harrow Weald and Barking, before being withdrawn in 1979. (Peter Horner.

RT 2250 is blinded up for route 229, a route
that Bexleyheath lost in May 1977. On the left is
RT 4641, which displays the new style fleetname,
without the gold underlining. It is 28th June 1977.
(Mick Webber)

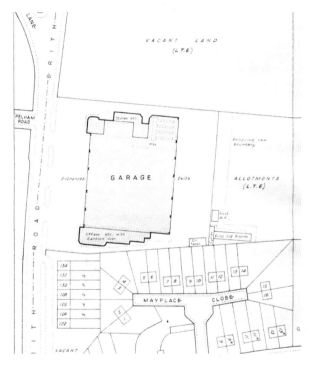

New styles at Bexleyheath. DMS 2399 was a 1977
delivery, and waits to proceed to Sidcup on the
269, whilst Titan T 743 arrived in 1983. Although
heavily damaged twice during the war, plus
two smaller bombing incidents, the depot was
faithfully rebuilt to retain its modern appearance,
with access doors across the whole frontage of
the building.

BOW (BW)

The LCC built a new tram depot at Fairfield Road, Bow in 1908 on the site of an old Asylum. The LPTB took over in July 1933, and eventually made the decision to replace trams with trolleybuses. This happened here in November 1939, and this form of transport ruled until they, in turn, were replaced by buses on 19th August 1959. RTLs were used initially, and when nearby Clay Hall garage closed in November 1959, Bow received an allocation of RTWs. RTs came in 1968, and Routemasters arrived in 1965 (RM) and 1975 (RML). The first of the ill-fated DMS class were drafted in during 1972. Bow shared the special Port of London route with Athol Street, and later Poplar, until that was withdrawn in 1969. Routes operated at April 1983 were 8, 8A, 10 and 25. The garage is still in operation.

Left: The grand LCC style frontage at Bow that has hosted trams, trolleybuses and buses, has not been changed or modified since it was built in 1908. This February 1976 view shows Seven Kings RT 2201 emerging after turning short here on route 86. (Peter Horner)

Above: The highest numbered of its class, RTL 1631, was at Bow for its last year of service from September 1967 until September 1968. It is parked here next to two RTW trainers, the nearest of which is RTW 69. (Peter Horner)

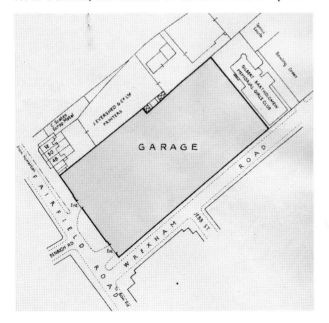

RTL 1579 is a West Ham vehicle arriving on a short working of the 25, and enters the portal at the garage showing Bow Church, which was the run-in display. (Mick Webber)

BRIXTON (BN)

Streatham tram depot had been built in 1892 as a cable car shed. It began operating electric trams in 1906, and was expanded in 1911, when a second shed was added. It was renamed Brixton in 1950. Trams were withdrawn on 6th January 1951, and as the existing structure was unsuitable for conversion to buses, the substantial buildings were demolished. The new garage was far from ready to operate the replacement RTs, and an open space behind Streatham Hill Theatre was used for parking. The complete allocation at Brixton was not fully operational until November 1953. During the early 1960s, RTs were replaced by RTLs and RTWs, only to return in 1965. Routemasters came in 1966, and the last RTs left in 1976. Brixton was the last garage to operate RTWs in London, and was one of the first two garages to work the new DMS class in 1971 on route 95. Routes operated at April 1983 were 50, 95, 109, 118, 133, 159 and N87. The garage still operates.

The aspect of Brixton garage as seen from Streatham Hill. The site was originally divided in two by a Metropolitan Water Board water main, which was straddled by two tram sheds. After an agreement, this was resolved, and the new garage built. The block in the centre houses the offices and canteen. (LTM)

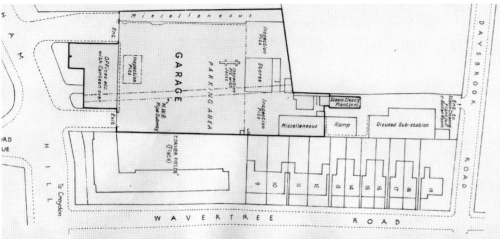

Looking at the left hand side of Brixton garage in 1960. The trainer on the left is RT 63, and on the right is RT 1363, ready and waiting to operate a Chelsea football extra, once a common sight on a Saturday. (Terry Cooper Collection/Mick Webber)

BROMLEY (TB)

The garage at Bromley was originally used by Thomas Tilling, and opened on 15th April 1924. The allocation of Tilling style STs and STLs worked from here, and also in 1949, some pre-war AEC Regents were hired from Leeds Corporation and used until June 1950. RTs first appeared in 1948, and remained until 1978. A few RTWs arrived in June 1950, but were gone by March 1951. Single deck LTs and later

RFs worked on route 227. The one man era with MBs, SMSs and DMSs started in 1971 and 1972. Routemasters didn't feature here until 1975. By the early 1980s, a yard was opened up on the north side of Lower Gravel Road, which was used as a parking area and storage space. The garage remains open. Routes operated at April 1983 were 47, 61, 119, 119B, 126, 138, 146, 227, 261 and B1.

Catford RT 708 is leaving Bromley garage for Shoreditch on route 47 in the early 1960s. The garage looks smartly maintained, with its advertisement panels all neatly displaying London Transport posters. The garage had a maximum use for 86 buses in 1960. (Terry Cooper Collection/Mick Webber)

Compare this 1980 view with the earlier shot, and it is apparent just how much more cluttered the place is. Cars are now parked on the pavement outside the garage, the London Transport bronze plate by the door is gone, and there is now an inspectors hut. Dalston RM 1989 leaves on the 47 after a break. (John Gillham)

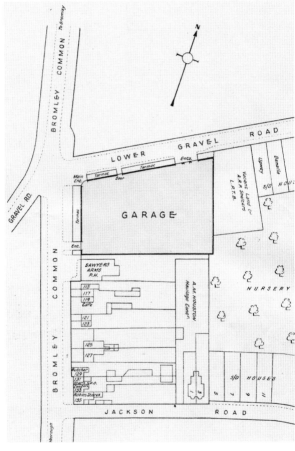

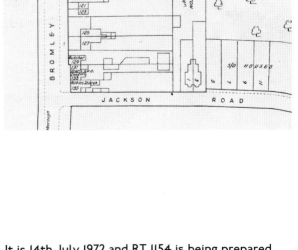

It is 14th July 1972 and RT 1154 is being prepared for sending off to Aldenham for a repaint later that month. SMS 322 keeps it company in this view. (Peter Horner)

CAMBERWELL (Q)

The garage at Camberwell was opened on 29th June 1914. It was closed during the first war from 12th November 1914 until 8th July 1919. Body overhauls were carried out here during 1940 and 1941, and in 1943, it operated the first gas fuelled buses. A mix of NS, ST and STLs were operated in the late 1930s. RTLs came here in 1950, and also some SRTs were used. The first Routemasters arrived in 1965, and RTs replaced the Leylands in 1966. The one man Fleetlines ousted the RTs in 1975, and new Titans were taken into stock in 1982. The single deck operation was small, and MBs and SMSs worked during the 1970s. A major building project in 1951, saw a new docking unit installed, and the running shed enlarged. This enabled Camberwell to carry out its responsibilities for heavy maintenance to its own buses, and those from Walworth and Battersea. Routes operated at April 1983 were 3, 35, 42, 68, 159, 172, 188 and 196. The garage is still in operation.

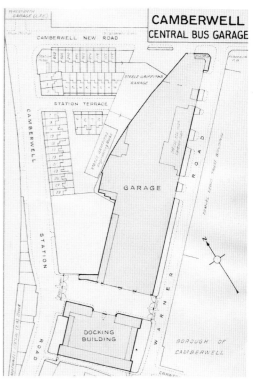

The main office building at Camberwell, at the junction of Camberwell New Road, and Warner Road on the left. The canteen was situated on the left hand side of the garage in Warner Road. (LTM)

Above: The new docking unit built in 1951. Major work for Camberwell, Walworth and Battersea was carried out here. The building was separated from the main garage by a service road, which linked Warner Road with Station Road. (LTM)

Below: This is the extension of the running shed built in 1951 pictured in 1954. RTLs form the whole allocation at this time, and the maximum daily vehicle requirement was 163.

CARSHALTON (CN)

Sutton tram depot was opened by the South Metropolitan Electric Tramways and Lighting Company in 1906. London Transport converted it to trolleybus operation in 1935, and in July 1950, it was renamed Carshalton, to avoid confusion with Sutton bus garage when the Central Buses and Tram and Trolleybus departments were merged. When the trolleybuses were replaced on 4th March 1959, RT buses took over, and remained the only type of vehicle operated by this garage. It had the smallest allocation of buses in the central area, and it was therefore no surprise when it was closed on 29th January 1964, and routes 154 and 157 transferred to Merton and Sutton. The building still exists and is in use as a storage facility. Maximum vehicle requirement was 25 at time of closure.

This nice sunny view shows Carshalton garage on 21st September 1960. Just over a year since the final trolleybuses had run here, the garage still retains many of the RTs that were first drafted in, a lot of which had roof box bodies. Its use as a bus garage was short, and lasted just under five years. The building still exists and is in use as a self-storage depot (LTM)

The garage operated Christmas day extras on trolleybus route 630, between Mitcham and West Croydon, and after Carshalton lost its trolleybuses in March 1959, they worked the extras with RTs, although the 630 route number was not shown. Christmas day 1959 was the only year that this occurred, as route 630 was withdrawn in 1960. RT 543 leaves the garage to take up duty. (Alan Cross)

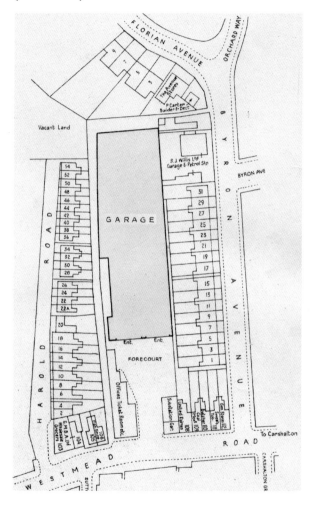

Changeover on 3rd/4th March 1959. A redundant B1 class trolleybus number 67 stands over the pit, whilst RT 2636 stands on the soon to be removed turntable, ready for route 157. The depot only operated one route, the 654, and replacements would be on altered route 157 and new route 154. (Alan Cross)

CATFORD (TL)

Thomas Tilling operated from the garage that was built in Bromley Road, and opened on 11th May 1914. It replaced Tilling's smaller premises in Lewisham. The building was closed during the first war on 23rd January 1915, and didn't reopen until 3rd October 1920. In the mid-1930s ST and STLs made up the allocation with a few T types. It received its first RTs in 1948, and in 1954, had nearly 200 of the class.

An RT allocation continued until 1978. Routemasters were introduced in 1968, and one man type single and double deckers of the SM, SMS and DMS classes came in the period 1970-72. Titans made their appearance in 1983. The garage has been enlarged over the years, and was modernised in 1970. It remains open. Routes operated at April 1983 were 1, 47, 54, 75, 108B, 124, 124A, 160, 160A, 180, 185 and 208.

Catford garage from Bromley Road in April 1936. The standard London Transport notice board layout can be seen on the right, complete with timetables and bus maps, and people wait at the "tombstone" style bus stop.

Six buses occupy the maintenance area at Catford in April 1936. From left to right are two Tilling STs, STL 498, another Tilling ST, a standard ST and STL. Four members of staff have the attention of the camera man as he records the scene. (LTM)

Catford shared route 185 with Walworth, and in this May 1973 view, RT 2877 is leaving to take up the route at Catford Church. The forecourt was used to store buses overnight, although the situation was eased when extra space was provided on the south side of the site on land previously occupied by car dealer Stewart and Ardern, whose premises can be seen here in the distance. (Peter Horner)

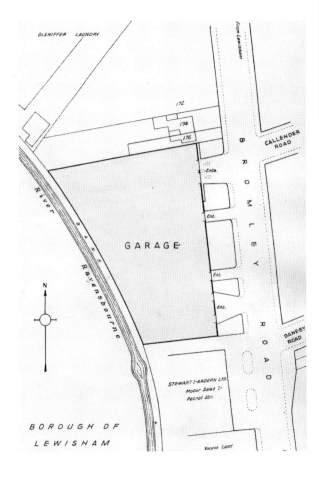

Catford garage on 15th April 1978. The forecourt here was used by many terminating buses, and New Cross RM 155 is just leaving on route 1 whilst Plumstead RT 2690 waits at the door next to home RT 1152. One of the garage's DMSs can be seen on the right. (Mick Webber)

This garage was opened on 6th March 1916, replacing an earlier location in Albany Street that was requisitioned during the first war. Some body overhauls were carried out here during 1940/41. STLs formed the main allocation in the mid-1930s with some single deck Q types. The first post-war buses to work from here were SRTs in 1949, and these were joined in 1950 by RTLs and RTWs. Some RTWs were used on route 31 in May 1950 in trials to prove the 8 feet wide vehicles were suitable for central London operations. The Leyland's remained after the demise of the SRTs, until they were joined in 1963 by Routemasters. The first experimental XA class Atlanteans worked from here in 1965 on route 24, and the RTWs were replaced. The XAs lasted until 1966, when they were ousted by RMLs. The RTLs were superseded by RTs in 1966, and the eventual one man wave of new buses in the form of the DMS took hold in 1972. A notable event took place in 1976, when the prototype "B15" Titan was allocated here, and worked on route 24. Loss of tendered routes led to its closure on 30th July 1993, with work being transferred to Holloway (HT). Routes operated at April 1983 were 3, 24, 46, and 68. New housing now occupies the site.

The garage exterior on Harmood Street at Chalk Farm in August 1936. The site has since been cleared, and housing now occupies the area. (LTM)

A wonderful assortment of vehicles in the maintenance area at Chalk Farm on 26th August 1936. Three men give attention to STL 458, whilst others attend to NS 1085. Next is NS 123 standing alongside an unidentified Q type single decker. STLs 462, 437 and 497 all from the 1934 batch are next in the line-up, with NS 1629 at the end. (LTM)

Park Royal-bodied D 1102 and MCW-bodied DMS 1851 were allocated to Chalk Farm, and are seen next to RM 1413. Note the run in display for route 46 was "Prince of Wales Road, Harmood Street" (Peter Horner)

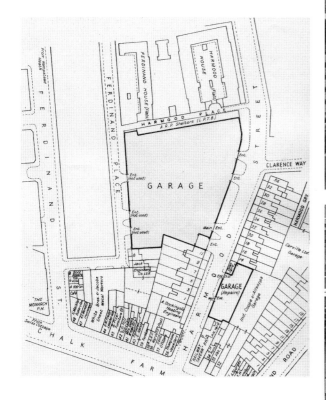

RM 1528 was a resident at Chalk Farm for just over four years and heads a line-up of RMs blinded up for route 68, a service it shared with Camberwell and Croydon. Both views taken on 24th April 1983. (Peter Horner)

CHISWICK (CS)

Although Chiswick was not an operational garage, it played a vital role in keeping London buses operating, and spare parts in constant supply. It was opened by the LGOC in August 1921, and as well as repairing and overhauling the fleet, it also built bus bodies. It was situated in Chiswick High Road, and covered a site of 32 acres.

A pre-war view taken in about 1938/39, showing LT 1311, built in May 1932, and STL 47, built in May 1933. Both had bodies built here, and look resplendent after their recent overhauls. 10T10 coach T 467 can be seen left of centre at the rear. (LTM)

A splendid line-up ready for service await inspection at Chiswick. New Ts 507 and 508 are on the left, and are next to LT 708, STL 47, LT 462 and ST 340. One of the many tractors used to manoeuvre the vehicles can be seen in front of the ST. (LTM)

CLAPHAM (CA)

The existing horse tram shed here was opened by the London Tramways Company in July 1888, and the LCC later converted and enlarged it to operate its electric service in 1903. When the tramway conversion started here, the shed began operating buses on 1st October 1950, and they worked alongside the trams until the final cars were withdrawn in January 1951, when it became a bus garage. RTLs were used until 25th November 1958, when it was closed. The maximum vehicle requirement at the time being 99. In March 1961, the building opened in a new guise, as the Museum of British Transport, a role it was to keep until 23rd April 1973. A second lease of life was to come on 25th April 1981, when it reopened as a bus garage as a base for the buses from Norwood, whilst that garage was rebuilt. When that task was complete, and Norwood's buses were returned, Clapham became host to the vehicles from Streatham, while that too was being rebuilt. Routes operated then were the 37 and 137 with a maximum vehicle requirement of 57 buses. During this period, Routemasters and Metrobuses were operated. When all of these rebuilding works were completed in 1987, Clapham closed its doors again, on 7th February. Routes operated at April 1983 were 37 and 137. A supermarket now occupies the site.

The entrance to Clapham garage from Triangle Place in the mid-1950s. The offices and canteen are in the block on the right. It only lasted just over seven years in its first life as a bus garage. (LTM)

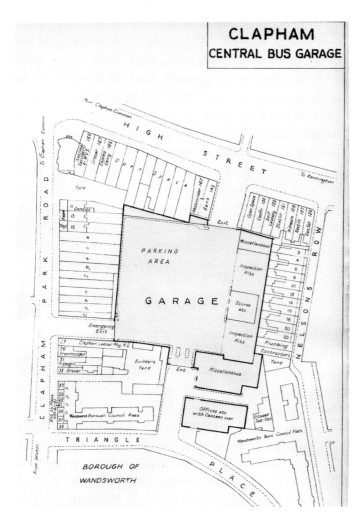

It is August 1954, and RTLs 1088 and 841 are prominent in this view of the garage. RTL 841 was one of the buses bodied by Metro-Cammell, which could be identified by the slightly thicker and heavier beading on the central relief band. (LTM)

The entrance to Clapham garage from the High Street. RTL 1020 is poised ready for route 189a at a time when the garage operated the type exclusively. When it closed in 1958, the work was transferred to Stockwell and Merton. The exit into Triangle Place can be seen in the background. (Norman Rayfield)

Right: Clapham during its second spell as an operational garage. The pit area is occupied by three Routemasters. RML 2351 is on the left, and RM 799 on the right, are being operated on behalf of Norwood, whilst that premises was being rebuilt. Extensive work was carried out here before reopening, which included the removal of some roof supports. (LTM)

CLAPTON (CT)

This shed was known as Hackney until the merging of the Bus and Tram and Trolleybus departments in 1950, when it was renamed to avoid confusion with nearby Hackney bus garage. It was originally a horse tram depot from 1883, but was acquired by the LCC and converted for electric tram operation in 1907. London Transport introduced trolleybuses here in 1939. After twenty years of service, the trolleybuses were replaced by buses in April 1959. Sixty seven RTLs were the first buses to work here; they were replaced by RTs in 1967, and they stayed until 1974. Routemasters first appeared in 1968, followed by DMSs in 1972 and Titans in 1982. The garage closed on 15th August 1987, but reopened in May 1989. It remains open. Routes operated at April 1983 were 22, 22A, 30 and 277.

Clapton by day and night. The daytime view was taken on 25th March 1967, and shows RTL 1475 waiting to enter after working on the 253A. Note the remaining tram track in the cobblestones. The night view, taken on the 17th of the same month, depicts RTL 536 in a similar position. Buses showed Hackney Station as a run in on their blinds. Roof box RTL 1475 appears again here, this time on the right, by the exit. (Mick Webber)

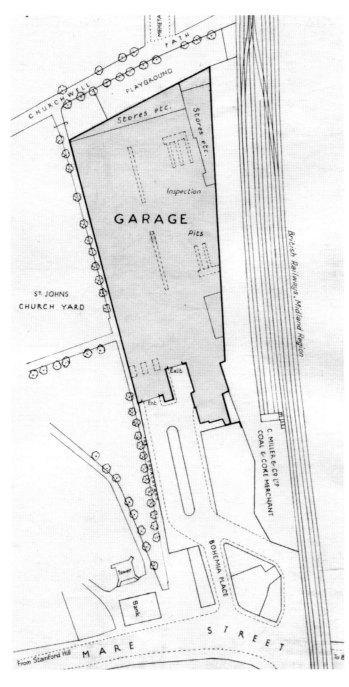

Over the pits at Clapton in January 1974 is RT 3336.
It has had its blinds removed in preparation for transfer
to Hendon later that month. All remaining RTs had left
by the end of that year. (Peter Horner)

CLAY HALL (CL)

A horse bus shed existed here from 1897, and this later became a bus garage from 31st October 1910 where the first B type buses operated. It closed between April 1917 and July 1919, and closed again on 10th January 1920. The site was cleared, and eventually a new garage was built opening on 7th October 1931, the LGOC working the first STL type from here in 1932. NS type buses initially came from Dalston. A café adjoining the right hand side of the garage, was damaged, along with some houses during the war, and when demolished in 1947, LT obtained permission to use the vacant land as an extension to the garage. Post war buses came with RTLs in 1950, and RTWs in 1951. In July 1950 some RTWs were used on routes 8 and 60 in trials to prove that the new 8 feet wide buses were suitable for central London work. The trials were a success. The garage suffered because of restrictive access due to low bridges, which prevented double deck buses gaining access to Bow Road. When the fourth stage of the trolleybus to bus conversion came in November 1959, it created space in nearby garages, making Clay Hall redundant. Most of its work was transferred to Bow, and the garage closed on 11th November 1959. Maximum vehicle requirement was 51. Routes worked were 8, 8A, 8B, 10, 25, 56 and the Port of London route. The whole site has since been redeveloped.

The garage from Old Ford Road. The code "Y" was originally used until the building shown here was built in 1931, and the code changed to "CL". On run in, buses showed Old Ford on their blinds. (John Gillham)

It is 2nd November 1959, and the garage at Clay Hall will be closed later that year. All of the buses in this view are RTWs, with RTW 307 at the forefront. Routes 8, 8A, 10 and 25 went to Bow, with workings on the 56 going to Athol Street. (LTM)

CRICKLEWOOD (W)

This site was originally a horse bus stables in 1898, and later became an LGOC motor bus garage, known as Dollis Hill, officially operational in May 1905. The General LS class worked from here in 1927, and the first LT in 1929, followed by STs and STLs. RTs came in 1948 followed by the hybrid SRT class in 1949. The SRTs left in 1954, and the RTs in 1962, being replaced by RTLs and some Routemasters. The prototype Routemaster RM1 first operated here in 1956 on route 2. RTLs left in 1968, and RTs returned until 1971. One man classes began to emerge in 1970 and 1971, when MB, MBS and SMs were drafted in alongside DMSs. The new LS class were allocated in 1978, and RMLs came in 1980. The garage was demolished, and a new facility created on the same site, opening in May 2007. Routes operated at April 1983 were 16, 16A, 32, 112, 240, 245, 266, 268 and N94.

The site at Cricklewood was triangular, and bounded on the left and right by railway lines. This view from the Edgware Road, was taken on 9th April 1967, and RTLs and a solitary RM are in attendance. The staff canteen was on the right by the Routemaster. (Mick Webber)

The south side at Cricklewood, often played host to withdrawn and stored vehicles. The former RT 106 was renumbered 1036TV and converted to a turnover bus in December 1955, for crews to practice their skills on lifting stricken buses. It spent most of its time at Cricklewood and Stonebridge Park, and was painted grey. One of the trolleybus recovery trucks is parked at the rear in this 1961 view. (Terry Cooper Collection/Mick Webber)

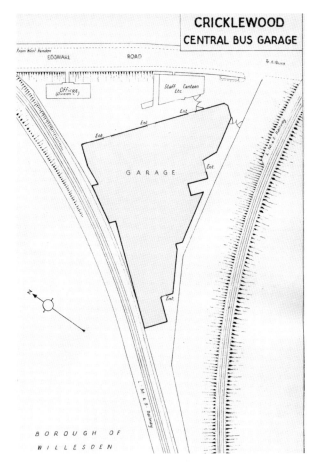

With stage 13 of the trolleybus conversion programme, Colindale trolleybus depot closed, and work was transferred to Cricklewood and Edgware. New Routemasters are in store here at Cricklewood waiting to take up their duties. RMs 1040, 1046 and 1041 are seen in this view taken a few weeks before the new services commenced on 3rd January 1962. (Terry Cooper Collection/Mick Webber)

CROYDON (TC)

Croydon was another of the garages used by Thomas Tilling, and opened on 23rd January 1916. London Transport's last open top buses, the STL type taken over from Charles Pickup, operated from here in 1934. A catastrophic bombing raid occurred here in May 1941, and 58 buses were destroyed, and four people killed. The garage was enlarged and completely rebuilt during the period 1952-1954. Post-war STDs were sent here before being transferred to Loughton in 1947, and then Croydon was one of the first garages to receive post-war RTs. Single deck LTs were replaced in 1953 by RFs. Routemasters arrived in 1964, with RMLs joining in 1967. One man double deckers featured in 1969 when the Atlantean XA type was allocated along with the front entrance Routemaster FRM 1. SMS class buses came in 1970, but these and the XA and FRM 1 were replaced by DMSs in 1973. RTs said farewell in 1974. An unusual event took place in 1975, when, owing to vehicle shortages, ten Leyland PD3s were hired from Southend Corporation, and worked on route 190. RFs left in 1977 to be replaced by BLs. The garage is still in operation. Routes operated at April 1983 were 68, 130, 130B, 157, 166, 166A, 190, 197, 234, and 234A.

This view was taken in April 1937. A group of busmen stand talking by the London Transport timetable board, and an open staircase Tilling ST can just be seen inside the right hand doorway. The vehicle turn out at this time was 92. (LTM)

Croydon garage as rebuilt, taken in the mid-1960s. Saunders RT 3275 has paused for a crew change on route 197, before preceding to Norwood Junction. (Terry Cooper Collection/ Mick Webber)

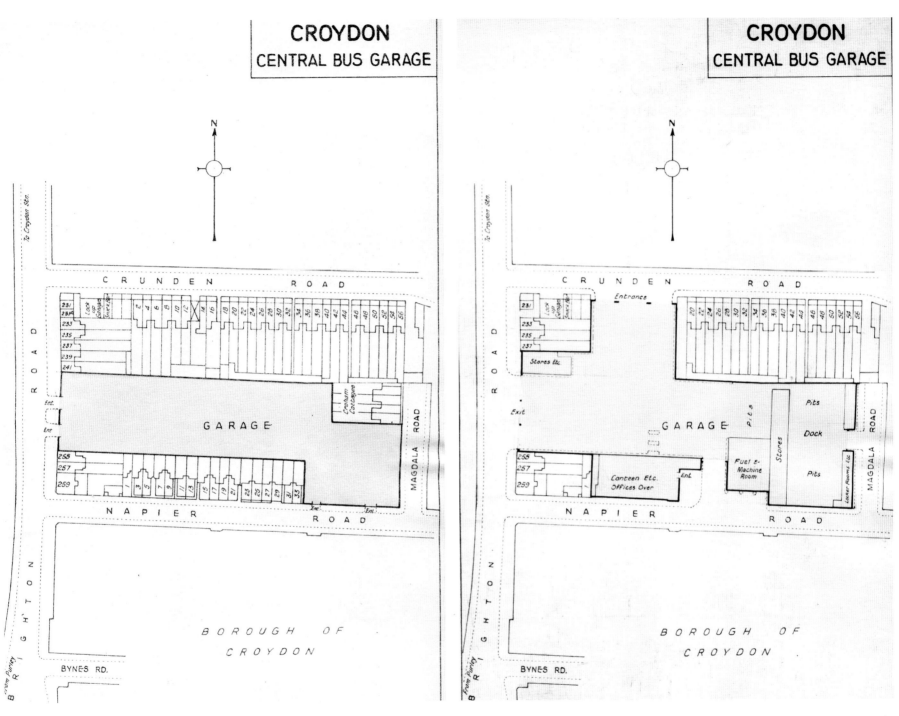

The original garage building, lost in bombing in 1941.

The garage as rebuilt after the war.

DALSTON (D)

The garage here is on a site of a former barracks, and it was used by the Pilot and Vanguard bus companies, before passing to the LGOC in 1908. It has long been associated with route 11, perhaps London's best known bus route. The garage overhauled mechanical units before Chiswick came on stream in 1921. Most pre-war classes worked from here including single deck LTs and Qs. The LTs were replaced in 1953 by RFs, which stayed until 1971. RTs were allocated in 1948 and RTWs in 1951. RTLs replaced the RTs in 1954, but the two types swapped again in 1968, the RTs staying this time until 1975. Three experimental lightweight single deckers were tried here in 1953-1954, they were an AEC Monocoach, a Leyland Tiger Cub, and a Bristol LS. The lowbridge RLH class worked from here on route 178 from 1959 until 1971. Routemasters first appeared in 1963, and stayed until closure. SMS vehicles were introduced 1971, and the first Leyland Nationals in 1973. Closure and replacement by Ash Grove came on 24th April 1981, and the garage has since been demolished. Maximum vehicle requirement at closure was 59, and routes worked were 9, 9A, 11, 47, 236, 253 and S2. New housing was subsequently built here.

Above right: The main entrance to Dalston garage in Shrubland Road. Its grand portal looks the worst for wear in this view of RT 1882 taken on 4th October 1969. The old "buses turning" sign can be seen on the left, and on the right a young boy looks on, perhaps a future bus spotter! (Peter Horner)

Right: The entrance in Ivydene Road nestles between Victorian terraced houses. With parked vehicles either side of the road, it was hardly suitable for manoeuvring buses, especially the longer more modern ones (John Gillham)

RTL 1607 was at Dalston for only nine months before being transferred to West Ham in June 1968. It is seen here on 27th January 1968, blinded up for the 47, a route it shared with Bromley and Catford. RM 1995 is on the left, and on the right are two RLHs. Eleven of this type were used on the Mon-Fri working of route 178. (Mick Webber)

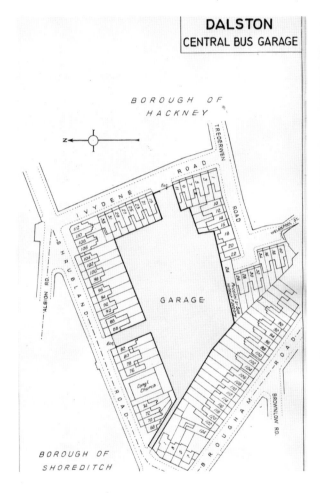

One of the jobs done in garages was the adding of 'inserts' to destination blinds where an additional display supplied by Aldenham was needed for a route. Two garage hands are seen doing this work in Dalston. (Capital Transport)

EDGWARE (EW)

The original garage built here opened on 8th April 1925, but only lasted until 1939, when a new structure was built and opened on 23rd January. STs, STLs and some single deck LTs were the initial allocation. The first post-war buses arrived in 1949 when RTWs and TDs were allocated. RTLs came in the mid-1950s, but the RT replaced them and remained until 1973. New DMS class buses then arrived and stayed until 1980 when the Metrobus took over their duties. The TDs had earlier been superseded by RFs in 1962 and remained until 1977. One man SMS class buses also appeared here in 1970. The garage was demolished and replaced by a new building in 1984, which remains operational. Routes operated at April 1983 were 142, 186, 240, 251, 286, 288 and 292.

The second structure built in 1939 seen in May 1954. One of the single deck TDs used on route 240A is parked inside. The long approach Road from the main Station Road can be seen in the foreground. (LTM)

An interesting scene from about 1960. TD 89 is in the foreground and a maximum of ten of these were needed to operate route 240a. RT 2735 can be seen just inside the garage on the left, and a pre-war RT trainer on the right just behind the TD. (Terry Cooper Collection/Mick Webber)

EDMONTON (EM)

The tram depot here was originally for horse trams from 1881, and later steam trams from 1885. It was converted for electric operation by the Metropolitan Electric Tramways in 1905. London Transport changed over to trolleybuses in 1938. When the trolleybus to bus conversions came in April 1961, the two types of vehicles worked side by side for a few months until buses took over completely in July. New Routemasters were allocated, and remained until closure. The DM and DMS classes came here in 1973/4, and also the RCLs repurchased from London Country worked between 1980 and 1984. The Fleetlines were replaced by the Metrobus in 1982. Some of the garage space was used as a store for the building department for the Victoria Line in the 1960s. The garage closed on 1st February 1986. Routes operated at April 1983 were 144A, 149, 279, 279A and W8. New housing now occupies the site.

Right: New RMs 718 and 725 parked and ready for service on the new trolleybus replacement services 279 and 127 at the first of two stages of the conversion programme here in April 1961.

Below: RM 1225 inside Edmonton on 23rd April 1977. The bus was in a five year period of allocation here from March 1974 until March 1979. (Peter Horner)

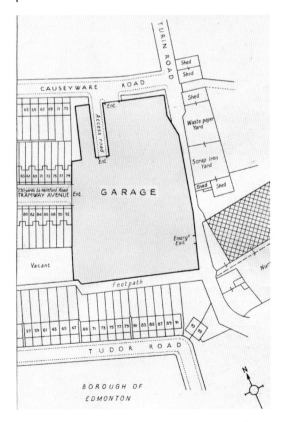

The front of Edmonton garage was plain and simple. It stood at the end of Tramway Avenue, and had been extensively rebuilt in 1938 to accommodate trolleybuses, the small forecourt that existed being covered. RM 148 leaves on the 279, former trolleybus route 679, in this 1977 view. (Peter Horner)

ELMERS END (ED)

The garage at Elmers End was opened on 27th March 1929. NS types were used here and later STs and STLs. By the time war commenced, the allocation comprised mainly of single and double deck LTs. Tragedy struck in July 1944, when a flying bomb killed ten staff and destroyed 32 buses. The garage was completely rebuilt and reopened on 14th May 1954, and incorporated a plaque in memory of the wartime dead. The post–war period saw RTs arrive in 1948 gradually taking over, apart from the allocation of ten STLs to work the special Festival of Britain services in 1951. Some RTWs took part in a one week experiment in May 1950, when they worked from here on the 12, to prove that 8 feet wide buses could safely operate on central routes. The RT dominated until 1973, apart from a brief interlude with RMs in the early 1960s for route 64. Routemasters returned in 1973 with DMSs, replacing the RT. SMS class buses came in 1970, and were duly ousted by the LS in 1977. The garage was closed on 24th October 1986, and subsequently demolished to make way for housing. Routes operated at April 1983 were 12, 12A, 54, 194 and 289.

A view of Elmers End garage from Elmers End Road. After the wartime bombing, the staff had suffered for ten years without full garage facilities, and with street parking for many buses the local residents were not too happy either. It was therefore a great relief when the new garage opened in 1954. The garage entrance is on the left, with the offices and first floor canteen in the main building. (Gerald Mead)

RT 1809 stands at the exit in Beck Lane on 25th August 1967, ready for route 12. This exit was named the "Cunningham gate" in memory of the fire watcher who was killed after warning of the flying bomb approach. (Peter Horner)

RT 2653 arrived at Elmers End after overhaul in March 1968 and stayed until withdrawn in January 1973. It is going through the bus wash in this view, with the Elmers End Road entrance in the background. (LTM)

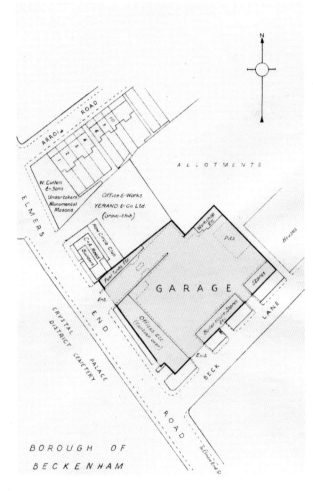

A line-up at Elmers End in the early eighties. From left to right are LS 114, and RMs 2177, 432, 2061 and 664. Twenty six Routemasters were used for peak requirement on route 12 at this time. (Peter Horner)

ENFIELD (E)

This garage was built by the LGOC and leased to the London Public Omnibus Company. It opened on 23rd May 1928, and became an LGOC shed when Public lost control in December 1929. The garage is actually in Ponders End, and buses show this on their blinds when running in. The large forecourt here was wired up for trolleybuses to terminate between 1938 and 1961. In early years, STLs, LTs and single deck Ts and Cs were operated, and later utility Guys came here in large quantities. In the early period after the war, many types appeared here including RT, RTL, RTW, STD, G, T and TD. The RTL and RTWs were replaced in 1952 with RTs which worked here until 1978. Routemasters appeared in 1968, and DMSs in 1972, which in turn gave way to Metrobuses in 1981. RF single deckers came in 1966 and MB and MBS types in 1970 being replaced by the SMS. A major modernisation and extension took place in the early 1980s. The garage still operates. Routes operated at April 1983 were 107, 121, 191, 217, 217B, 231, 279, 279a and W9.

A view of the garage at Ponders End in the early LPTB period. Trolleybus overhead was installed here in 1938 to allow terminating trolleybuses which travelled in from the Hertford Road. (LTM)

The date is 25th March 1967, and once again, RTs dominate. Solitary RF 480 is on the left blinded up for route 121, and RTs 480 and 1546 are identifiable. A mark one Ford Cortina occupies the bus wash. (Mick Webber)

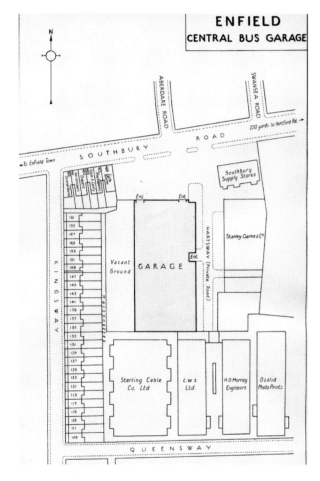

Park Royal bodied RT 3350 sits inside Enfield garage on 11th April 1959; in two months' time it would go to Aldenham for overhaul. All vehicles in this view are of the RT class, which dominated, working routes 102, 102A, 107, 107A, 121, 128, 135, 191, 205, 217, 231, 242 and 242A. (Alan Cross)

FINCHLEY (FY)

The depot in Woodberry Grove was built in 1905 by the Metropolitan Electric Tramways Company, and it was enlarged and extended in 1912 and 1930. London Transport converted it to trolleybus operation in 1936. When the trolleybuses were replaced by buses here, there was a transitional period between November 1961 and January 1962, when both types were worked. When trolleybus route 609 was replaced by new bus route 104, the new RML type was first introduced when they were allocated here along with standard Routemasters. RTs also worked here, and by 1971 the SMS, and in 1972 the DMS arrived replacing Routemasters. The RML re-appeared in 1978, and Metrobuses came in 1980. The Transit mini-buses were introduced for the Hampstead dial-a-ride service in 1974. The loss of tendered routes made the garage surplus to requirements, and it was closed on 4th December 1993. Routes operated at April 1983 were 13, 26, 43, 125, 221 and H2. A superstore was built on the site.

The garage from Woodberry Grove. Route 125 used the forecourt here as a terminus, and Finchley's own RT 2205 stands before returning to Southgate Station. (Peter Jones)

The new RML class was first tried here when they replaced trolleybuses on route 609 in November 1961. They worked new route 104, and three of the class, RMLs 883, 880 and 882, are seen here prior to entry into service. The trolleybus turntable can just be seen in the foreground. (Norman Rayfield)

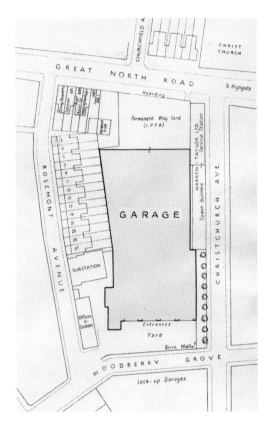

Inside Finchley in June 1981. RML 2409 has its back to the camera and RML 2602 is facing in the distance. Routemasters had left the garage in 1972, but were re-introduced in 1978. It was now common practice for staff to park their cars inside the garage. (Peter Horner)

FOREST GATE (G)

The premises here was originally owned by the Great Eastern London Suburban Tramways & Omnibus Company, and was used as a horse bus base from 1898. It was first opened as a motor bus garage on 26th March 1906, and was subsequently taken over by the LGOC May 1911. Most standard LGOC types worked from here in pre-war years, and the double deck TD type was here in the early London Transport years. Post war, some SRTs worked on route 66, and in 1950, new RTs were allocated for the 25B. The trolleybus conversion programme freed up much space at nearby West Ham, and on 26th April 1960, Forest Gate was closed, most of its work being transferred to WH, with some to North Street and Upton Park. The garage front has since been preserved, and a shopping arcade has been built inside. Maximum vehicle requirement for 1959 was 67, and routes operated were 25, 66 and 145.

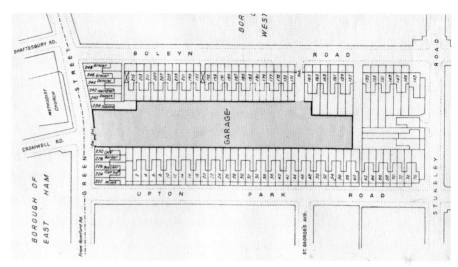

A view of the garage from Green Street in 1936. A rather modest entrance disguises a large garage surrounded on three sides by terraced housing, and at this time having a maximum requirement of 129 buses at peak times. (LTM)

A splendid pre-war line of buses inside Forest Gate. STL 267 is just seen on the left. The line-up shows, from right to left, STL 482, TDs 42, 21 and 115, followed by two more STLs and STL 254, an LT and STL 541. A further TD and LT can also be seen along with two NSs. (LTM)

Another pre-war view showing STLs 1166, 481, 473, NS 1372, LT 936 and STL 334. The NS and the LT are receiving attention, and the NS would soon be withdrawn from service with the rest of its class. (LTM)

FULWELL (FW)

This large depot was built by the London United Tramways in 1903. They introduced the first London trolleybuses here in May 1931, and London Transport completed the conversion from trams in 1935. An overhaul facility existed here for the trolleybus fleet, and occupied the south side of the depot. It was the last depot to operate trolleybuses, when they were withdrawn on 8th May 1962, and replaced by Routemasters. RFs were also introduced to operate route 206. This arrangement continued until 1970, when closure of Twickenham garage brought some RTs and SMs. DMSs came in 1972, and RTs were replaced. The DMS class were in turn moved on to be replaced by the Metrobus in 1979, and single deck types included the SMS, SMD and BL, with LSs appearing in 1978. The two access points from Wellington Road and Stanley Road were reduced to one, when the Stanley Road entrance was taken out of use, this and part of the old overhaul works being isolated from the main building, and transferred to a private company. Routes operated at April 1983 were 33, 90B, 110, 267, 270, 281, 285 and 290.

The impressive frontage of Fulwell garage on 29th April 1967. Its tramway heritage is obvious, and much of the track work still exists in the cobblestones, and the tram road track numbers are still in situ above the doors. A relic of the trolleybus days can be seen on the left where a former trolleybus traction standard has been used as a lamp support. RMs 1086 and 1119 are parked facing Wellington Road, and the former overhaul part of the garage is on the right, by now in private hands. (Mick Webber)

Inside Fulwell on 29th April 1967, and RTWs 259 and 467 are parked at the rear of the garage. RTW 259 was a trainer based at Twickenham, and RTW 467 was by now privately owned and in preservation, being the last RTW to operate in service. (Mick Webber)

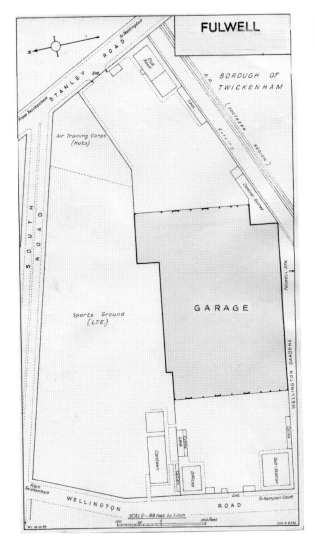

New Metrobus M 28 inside Fulwell in March 1979. The first fifty five of the class had the white upper deck relief. It was one of a large allocation of the class to Fulwell. (Peter Horner)

HACKNEY (H)

The LGOC opened Hackney garage on 6th July 1911. The garage was originally hidden behind shops and houses in Well Street with a narrow access road, but London Transport acquired the land between the garage and the main road, and it was cleared to allow the garage to be extended towards to road, and eventually covered to provide space for the extra buses now allocated for the increased work on route 42. This work was completed in 1938. At the outbreak of war, the entire allocation was STL. After the war, RTs arrived in 1950 and RTWs in 1951. Some RTWs came here in May and June 1950 to take part in trials on routes 6 and 22, to test the suitability of 8 feet wide buses in central London. RTLs replaced the RTs in 1952, although the RT did return in 1968. RMs in 1964 and RMLs in 1966 joined the allocation, and eventually the one man DMS came in 1972, only to depart in 1979. MBA vehicles started to work Red Arrow routes from here in 1968. At closure, which came on 25th April 1981, the stock was of Routemaster and MBA types. Routes worked at the time were 6, 30, 35, 106 and 502 and 75 vehicles were operated. A supermarket now occupies the site.

Below: A view of Hackney garage in the early 1980s. The garage was used for terminating buses, and RM 1933 and RM 866 are standing on routes 35 and 6. A fibreglass inspectors hut can be seen on the left. The garage has since been demolished and a supermarket occupies the site. (Capital Transport)

Below right: RT 3961 was a Clapton bus when this view was taken in December 1971, so the bus was probably in for maintenance. Open pits were commonplace at the time, before health and safety rules were fully implemented.

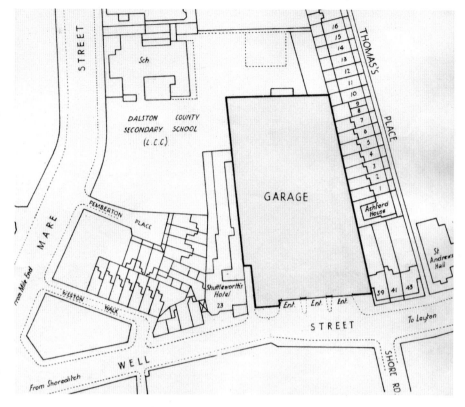

HANWELL (HL)

The tram depot on this site was built by the London United Tramways in 1901. London Transport completely rebuilt the shed in 1936 with a new access being provided in Jessamine Road, and it began trolleybus operation in that November. Their reign came to an end when they were replaced by new Routemasters on 9th November 1960. RTs were introduced between 1963 and 1965, and then RMLs began to appear in 1968 with some MBSs. 1975 saw the DMS and SMS classes arrive although the SMSs were replaced by LSs in 1978. The DMSs left when new Metrobuses came in 1981. Routemasters left in 1987. The garage was closed on 27th March 1993, demolished in 1996 and replaced by a supermarket. Routes operated at April 1983 were 207, E1, E2, E3 and N89.

The main forecourt at Hanwell. In trolleybus days the last section of the building on the left was a tower wagon shed. Terminating buses on the 255 stood here, and just emerging from the garage is trainer RTW 271, which had been withdrawn from service work in January 1965. (Peter Jones)

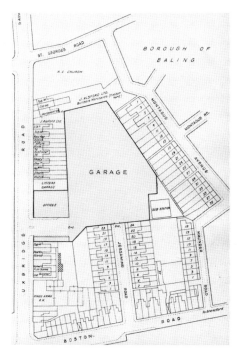

The bus wash area at Hanwell in February 1976. RML 2633 approaches with its number plate hanging down in need of attention. On the right is new DM 1213 which had just been delivered here. (Peter Horner)

HARROW WEALD (HD)

This was one of the last new garages built by the LGOC, opening on 9th February 1930. There was originally a large forecourt here, but this was later covered in 1932 to enlarge the garage. The first three diesel engine buses in London, which were STs, were based here. The pre-war allocation was of the ST, STL, Q and C classes. Low-bridge STLs came during the war years for route 230, and these were replaced in 1952 by the new RLH class. In 1949, new RTWs, SRTs and TDs came, although the RT took over double deck work in 1951. This allocation continued until 1978 when RMs first arrived. The RLH disappeared in 1969 with MBSs being transferred in. A couple of RFs came in 1966 for new route 136, and they stayed until 1971. New MBs and SMSs arrived in 1970 and 1971, and LS class buses took over single deck work in 1978. Routemasters left in 1983, and the Metrobus came on the scene: The garage is still in operation. Routes operated at April 1983 were 114, 136, 140, 209, 258 and H1.

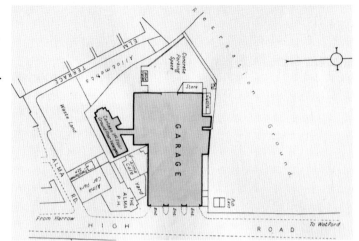

The frontage at Harrow Weald on the High Road. Open space at the rear was enlarged in 1970, . The area in this view was once part of a forecourt, before being covered in 1932. (Gerald Mead)

RT 684 and RT 2057 are terminating buses on routes 209 and 230A. The latter was a short local route requiring just two RTs and was withdrawn in January 1966.

Two RFs were needed to work local route 136, and RF 516 is the spare bus seen in this February 1967 view. In the background to the right are RTL 1332 and RT 2505. The RTL was the Cricklewood staff bus at this time, so its attendance here is unknown. (Mick Webber)

HENDON (AE)

This LGOC garage opened on 8th March 1913, and was the first to provide the staff with recreational facilities. ST, STL and NS types worked here, but in 1937 it was to be the first home to the pre-war STD class buses, which provided its backbone until 1952. In 1951 and 1952 RTLs and RTs arrived and the last STD departed in 1954. The RTL allocation lasted only a few months. Routemasters appeared in 1962, and the last RTs went in 1975. The DMS worked here from 1975 and RMLs were allocated from 1976. The DMSs were replaced by Metrobuses in 1980, and the garage closed on 5th June 1987, work passing to Harrow Weald, Edgware and Holloway. Routes operated at April 1983 were 113, 143 and 183.

Left: The frontage of Hendon garage on The Burroughs, taken in 1967. The LGOC stone plaque at roof level denotes the year of construction. A memorial to staff lost in the World Wars can be seen between the two lower windows on the left. (Mick Webber)

Above: RT 311 is parked in the doorway to The Burroughs in April 1967. The bus was to go for overhaul in June. An RTW trainer can be seen in the background, with an RM by the bus wash. Several RTLs were being prepared for shipment to Sri Lanka here at this time. (Mick Webber)

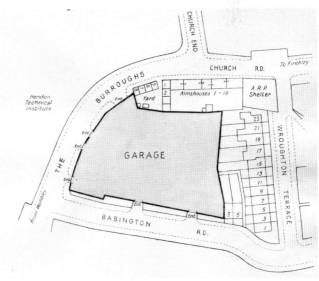

HIGHGATE (HT)

This was built as Holloway tram depot by the LCC between 1907 and 1909. It was the only shed north of the river to retain trams throughout the war years and up to April 1952. Trolleybuses began replacing trams here in March 1938 but the full conversion was suspended after declaration of war. After hostilities, trams and trolleybuses worked side by side until the final Kingsway Subway tram routes were withdrawn in April 1952. The depot was renamed Highgate in 1950 to avoid confusion with the nearby Holloway bus garage. The trolleybus to bus conversions brought Routemasters to Highgate in July 1960, and the gradual replacement took until April 1961, when buses took over completely. A brief interlude between 1963 and 1965 saw RTLs make an appearance, but these were replaced by RTs. The XA and XF types came in 1965/6 for evaluation trials, and were superseded in 1968 by RMLs. MBs worked here and, for a short spell, some RFs. The closure of nearby Holloway (J) garage in 1971 made a big impact, and also new DMS and SMS types arrived. A big allocation of DMs came in 1975, and LSs appeared in 1978. Routemasters replaced the DMs in 1981. Routes operated at April 1983 were 4, 14, 19, 27, 29, 45, 74, 104, 214, 253, 271, C11, N92 and N93.

The main entrance at Highgate in Pemberton Gardens hides a huge space. After nearby Holloway bus garage closed in September 1971, there was a peak requirement of 210 buses here. (Peter White)

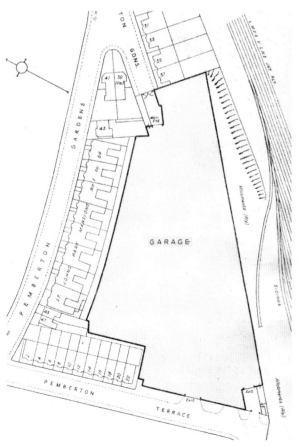

It is 10pm on 17th March 1967, and most buses have finished their work for the day. RM 425 and RML 2361 illustrate the changes made to the Routemaster front over the years. The RM displays the brake cooling grilles and number plate position along with the full depth ventilation grille between decks, whilst the RML has all of the modifications to these items. (Mick Webber)

HOLLOWAY (J)

This was originally a horse bus shed from the 1870s, and opened as a motor bus garage by the LGOC in October 1911. In the London Transport years up to the second war, ST, STL and single deck LTs worked from here with some of the LTC coaches. After hostilities, RTs came in 1948, and some SRTs in 1950, but RTs reigned until RMs arrived in 1963 and RMLs in 1967. In May and June 1950, it received some RTWs for a trial of the new buses on central London routes 14, 19 and 27a, to prove to the police that 8 feet wide vehicles could safely operate here. Prior to this, they were restricted to outer London routes only. The garage occupied an awkward triangular site, and unusually had the canteen built on a bridge over the entrance. Work was transferred to nearby Highgate, which was renamed Holloway, when it closed on 5th September 1971. Maximum vehicle requirement at closure was 87, and routes operated were 4A, 14, 19, 141A, 168A and 172. New housing was built here.

A view of the garage from beneath the bridge that served as a canteen. In this 1937 view, ST 628 stands in front of NS 2280 in the narrow service road that contained all five doors to the garage. (LTM)

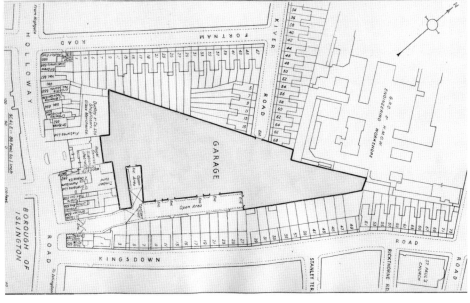

RT 2460 stands in the entrance to Holloway garage by the Holloway Road in 1960. The small access road belies the large garage that it led to, and after closure it became a bonded warehouse, before being demolished. Timothy Whites is one of many household names to have disappeared from our streets. (Terry Cooper Collection/Mick Webber)

HORNCHURCH (RD)

This garage was opened on 16th July 1924 as Romford, and was re-named Hornchurch on 1st September 1935. Its allocation in the mid-thirties consisted of ST, T, DA and single deck LTs. The STs were replaced by STLs in 1939, although the STs did return. C type Cubs also worked from here. After the war, utility Guys were allocated in 1947, and TDs arrived in 1948 for a ten year stay when, in 1958, all RD routes became double deck. RTLs had commenced work here in 1951 with some SRTs which lasted until 1953. The RLH started work here in 1955. In 1954, all of the RTLs were replaced by RTs, and in July 1966

the first RMs were received, followed in 1968 by the RML. The one man revolution reached Hornchurch in 1970 when SMS buses were drafted in followed in 1973 by the DMS, which made the garage the first central area shed to become all one man operated. The first Leyland Titans came here in 1978 for route 246, and later the LS took over single deck routes. The garage closed on 23rd September 1988. Routes operated at April 1983 were 165, 193, 244, 246, 248, 248A, 252 and 256. New housing was built here.

An interesting picture taken on 20th October 1936. Leyland Cub C51 is about to leave on route 252, with two T types and two STs in attendance on the left. A selection of staff notices can be seen on the far wall.

Hornchurch garage in 1967. The original building was extended in 1938, and a reconstruction carried out in 1954. The practice of parking cars on the pavement is very apparent. The garage has since been demolished to make way for housing. (Gerald Mead)

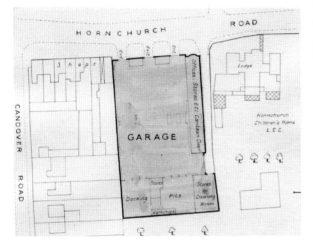

Two members of staff are in discussion next to RT 293 which looks ready for route 193. On the left is RLH 65, which is one of 5 of the type required to work the 248 and 248a in 1965. (Peter Jones)

HOUNSLOW (AV)

Hounslow Town Station once occupied the site where the LGOC built its garage at Hounslow. It was opened on 15th December 1913, but closed for a period during the first war between 31st January 1915 and 30th July 1919. London Transport demolished the old garage and built a new one on the site with adjoining land, and this opened in 1954. The first Leyland Cub, C1, worked here in 1934, and ST, LT, T and DA types all operated in the early LT days. RTs first came in 1948, with a few STLs, and RFs in 1952. RMs arrived in 1962 when nearby Isleworth trolleybus depot was closed, and the replacement buses operated from here. The RML joined the fleet in 1978, and the one man MB, SMS and SM classes appeared from 1969, being replaced by LSs in 1976. The RTs left in 1972 and the RFs in 1977. New Metrobuses came in 1982. Routes operated at April 1983 were 37, 81, 111, 116, 117, 202, 203, 237 and 257. The garage remains open.

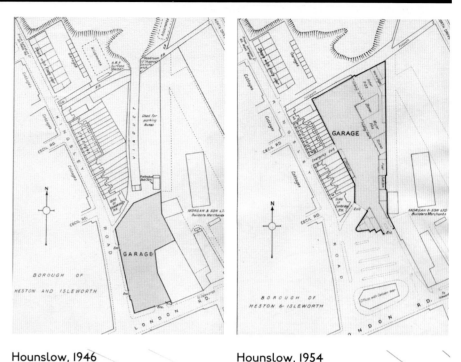

Hounslow, 1946   Hounslow, 1954

The original Hounslow garage as built by the LGOC, and pictured in November 1936. Trolleybus wires are in place for route 657, a route later replaced by bus 117, which would be operated by the new garage to be built here. (LTM)

Right: A 1961 view at Hounslow with RM 377 and RT 1166. The man on the left is selling football rosettes, and is hoping for custom from the travellers that will board football extras working from here later that day. (Terry Cooper Collection/ Mick Webber)

Below: Saunders RT 1696 rests at the new Hounslow garage in 1966 ready for service on route 203A. The bus station created here was built largely on the area previously occupied by the old garage. (Denis Battams)

Below right: An assortment of vehicles inside Hounslow garage. Thames Trader towing lorry 1240F from 1962, stands next to staff bus RT 4339 and RF 360 in this 1969 picture. The RT was delicensed later that year. (Peter Horner)

KINGSTON (K)

The garage here was opened on 4th January 1922 on Cromwell Road, but increased traffic made it necessary to build a bus station on Richmond Road in 1928, adjoining the site, and the two were connected. The garage always operated a large proportion of single deckers on rural routes. It received the first rear engine CR class in 1939, and also C class buses worked here. ST and single deck LT, Q and T types were the allocation in the immediate pre-war years. After the war, TD class vehicles arrived in 1949 along with some RTs, and in 1959, the RF started its long

association with the garage which lasted twenty years. A very brief RM allocation came in 1968, although they returned in 1978. Up until the opening of Norbiton garage in 1952, Kingston had to park some of its buses in a nearby car park and railway coal yard. It was the rebuilding of Norbiton in 1984 that brought about the closure on 3rd January 1984. It did reopen in June 1987 for Westlink services, but closed again in May 2000, and has since been demolished. Routes operated at April 1983 were 65 and 71. Commercial premises took over the site.

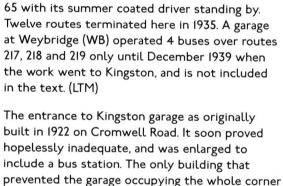

Kingston bus station in the mid-thirties. A Sutton single deck LT leaves on route 213 for Belmont, whilst Turnham Green ST 662 waits on route 65 with its summer coated driver standing by. Twelve routes terminated here in 1935. A garage at Weybridge (WB) operated 4 buses over routes 217, 218 and 219 only until December 1939 when the work went to Kingston, and is not included in the text. (LTM)

The entrance to Kingston garage as originally built in 1922 on Cromwell Road. It soon proved hopelessly inadequate, and was enlarged to include a bus station. The only building that prevented the garage occupying the whole corner site was the Kingston Cinema, the white building here on the right. (John Gillham)

The main allocation at Kingston in April 1967 when this view was taken, was the RF. Over thirty of them worked the OMO routes from here, and RF 523 is ready to leave on the 216 for Staines with RF 497 to the left. The advertisements in the background form the boundary between the garage and the bus station. (Mick Webber)

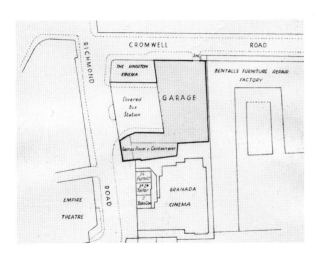

In the garage section at Kingston in 1977, RT 3951 is parked next to one of the BL class buses that came here in 1976. Their stay only lasted until 1982. A door marked "to the bus station" is on the far left, and the traffic office on the right. (Peter Horner)

LEYTON (T)

This LGOC garage was opened on 20th June 1912. In LT days, pre-war, the main allocation was of the ST and LT classes. The garage suffered serious bomb damage in 1940. It was the first garage to operate the post war RT in 1947 on route 10, and by the end of that year, over seventy were in stock. The class remained here until 1972. The single deck TD also worked here from 1949 until replaced by the RF in 1958. A few RTWs also made an appearance here between 1949 and 1951, and some took part in the trials for suitability of the new 8 feet wide vehicles in central London on routes 38 and 38a in June 1950 The Routemaster did not arrive here until 1966 (RML) and 1968 (RM). The new generation one man buses of MB, SMS and DMS classes eventually came in 1971 and 1972, followed by the LS in 1978. The garage was rebuilt and extended in 1959, and still operates. Routes operated at April 1983 were 38, 48, 55, 69, 97A, 230, 235, 236 and N96.

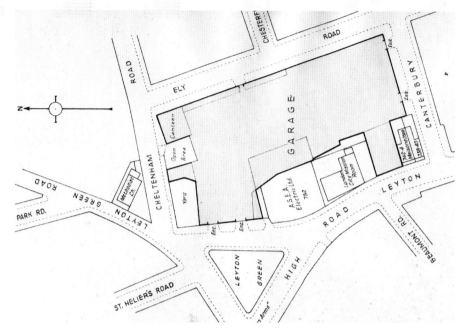

The garage front by Leyton Green with Cheltenham Road on the left. The busmen are wearing their summer white coats in this 1936 view. The garage was extensively damaged in 1940, and consequently partly rebuilt. The triangle at the front was later wired up as a trolleybus turning circle. (LTM)

RT 2554 arrived at Leyton in May 1977, and was moved on to Southall by September. RTs that worked the 230 from here had their front blind boxes masked to accept RM blinds. DMS 475 is poised by the bus wash. (Peter Horner)

LOUGHTON (L)

The LGOC garage here opened on 11th July 1923, and had the distinction of operating the first covered top double deckers in September 1925. The entire allocation comprised of open staircase LTs at one point, and then in the early post war period, it had an entire compliment of STDs. When new housing started to spread in the area, it was decided a new garage would be necessary, and one was built on the other side of the road. The old shed closed on 1st December 1953, with the new one opening the next day. It began with the STDs from the old garage, and then was the last garage to receive new RTs when the Leyland's were withdrawn in 1955. It never had any Routemasters. Single deck TDs came in 1954, but these were later replaced by RFs. The RTs were replaced by the DMS in 1976, which in turn were superseded by new Titans in 1982. MBs appeared in 1969, and SMSs in 1971. In 1976 the MBs and the RFs departed, followed by the SMS in 1978, being replaced by the LS. The death knell came when it lost most of its tendered routes, and it was closed on 24th May 1986, and subsequently demolished for housing. Ironically, the old garage still stands as part of a do-it-yourself store. Routes operated at April 1983 were 20, 167, 201, 206, 250 and 250A.

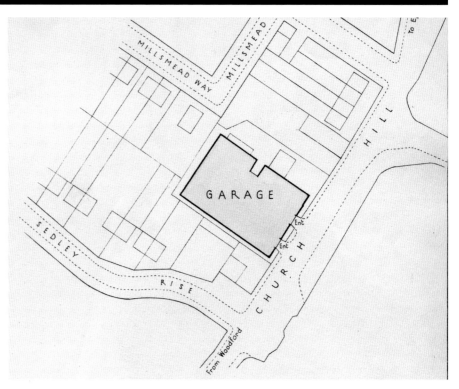

The old LGOC garage at Loughton on the west side of Church Hill. Ironically, the new garage on the opposite side of the road has disappeared completely, but the old one still survives behind a new front of a DIY store. (LTM)

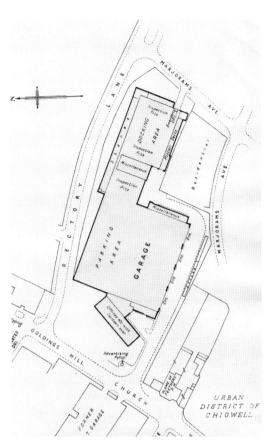

Loughton garage on 25th March 1967.

Above: The access road from Church Hill with a nice selection of staff cars.

Below: RTs 3880, 2186, 3063 and 1729 are visible in this view together with some of the RF allocation. The garage was always underused, and the large capacity was never realised, as the new estates planned for the area did not fully materialise. (Mick Webber)

MERTON (AL)

Merton garage was opened by the LGOC on 20th November 1913. London Transport allocated over two hundred STLs here in 1935, and although some LTs and NSs worked here, the STL was dominant until utility Daimlers arrived in 1944. The garage was later to operate all of this class totalling 181, until their demise in 1952/3. Single deck Q class buses were also operated. RTWs arrived for a one week experiment in May 1950 to prove to the police that 8 feet wide vehicles could safely work central London routes, and Merton used them on the 88. In 1953 over 100 new RTs arrived. The RLH came in 1952 to replace other lowbridge buses based here, and the RF took over from the Qs. RMs did not appear here until 1970, as did the MB class. The DMS and SMS were allocated in 1971, and gradually replaced the RTs which left in 1977. The garage was modernised in 1960. Routes operated at April 1983 were 49, 57, 77, 77A, 88, 127, 131, 152, 155, 156, 157, 189 and 200. It remains operational.

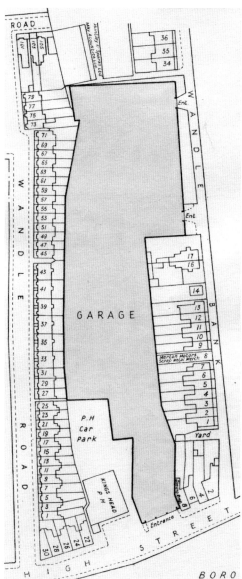

Merton garage side access in Wandle Bank in the 1930s. The original LGOC building on the left still stands, but the more austere corrugated iron section beyond has since been replaced by a modern two storey brick structure. (LTM)

The front of Merton garage has has changed little since the day it was built. These two views were taken in April 1967, when the run out was over 130 buses at maximum.

Below: It is midday, and the line-up here consists of RT 3698, RTW 79, RT 1626, RTW 67, RTW 469, RT 4303 and RT 1181. The three RTWs are trainers that were based here for a while. (Mick Webber)

MIDDLE ROW (X)

This back street garage was opened by the LGOC on 12th May 1910 occupying a corner plot between Middle Row and Conlan Street in North Kensington. In early LT days it worked ST and STL types, and after the war it received RTs in 1948, these being replaced by RTLs between 1955 and 1965, when the RTs returned. Some RTWs were drafted in for the May 1950 trials of the new 8 feet wide buses to prove their suitability on central London routes, the 28 being the route in question here. A few RTWs also worked here in 1958/9. RMs came as part of the trolleybus conversion scheme in 1962. RTs left in 1975 leaving RMs solely in charge until closure on 14th August 1981, with Westbourne Park opening the following day. The garage was rather cramped inside, and the narrow streets could not accommodate the bigger and longer modern buses. The building is still in use as industrial units.. Routes operated at time of closure were 7, 15, 18A, 28, 52 and 187 with vehicle requirement of 48.

The garage entrance in Middle Row. The building is run down and hardly looks fit to operate buses in this view. Very little has changed since the LGOC used to operate X and B type buses from here before the First World War. (John Gillham)

Taken on 2nd June 1981, just months before closure, this is Middle Row garage. Four Routemasters are lined up here, three of them are RMs 810, 1240 and 941, and as is usual by now, staff cars are parked within the garage. (LTM)

RTLs ruled when this view was taken in the 1960s. RTLs 1550 and 719 are seen here. RTL 719 is one of the Metro Cammell bodied buses, and is having rear panels replaced after an accident. (Robin Newell)

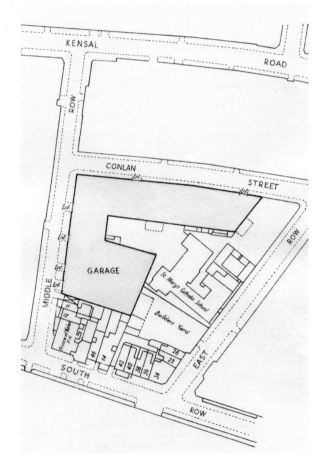

This scene dates from about 1980, and two Routemasters, RMs 200 and 144 form part of the allocation that were based here when the garage closed in August 1981. Like all of the others, they were transferred to the new garage at Westbourne Park. (Capital Transport)

MORTLAKE (M)

The site here was used as horse stables, and was built and opened as an LGOC bus garage on 9th July 1906. In London Transport days, most standard types were operated with over 80 buses required in the late thirties. RTs arrived in 1948, and were replaced by RTLs in 1955 which in turn were ousted by RMs from 1962. The Routemaster then worked exclusively from here until closure came on 25th June 1983. After closure and demolition, part of the site continued in use as a bus terminus for route 9, and the rest was for housing. Routes operated at April 1983 were 9 and 33.

A view from Avondale Road of the garage in 1936. Buses on route 9 turned here for many years, and after closure, work passed to Fulwell and Stamford Brook. The site was surrounded on all sides by terraced housing. (LTM)

The end aspect of Mortlake garage in North Worple Way taken from the railway footbridge. This end section now forms part of a bus stand, and new housing occupies the rest of the site. (John Gillham)

The docking area at Mortlake in June 1963. RMs 1325 and 1304 were from a batch delivered new here in December 1962, which started to replace the stock of RTLs. RM 1325 shows the offside route blind in use, and original front design, before later modifications. (LTM)

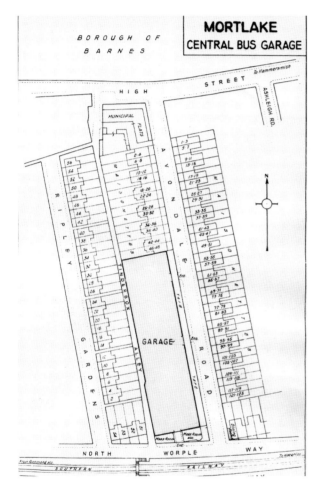

A view taken in 1980 when only Routemasters worked from here. RMs 1404, 1549 and 1623 all show route 9 blinds, the garage's main route which it had operated throughout the London Transport period. (Peter Horner)

MUSWELL HILL (MH)

Muswell Hill was one of the later LGOC garages, opening on 23rd September 1925. In LT days in 1937, it operated both single and double deck LTs. Body overhauls were carried out here during the early war years. After the war, the new TD class was first introduced here, and other single deckers in the early post war years included Ts and ex-Green Line Qs. It was the first garage to operate red RFs, which started to replace the older single deckers in 1952. RTs first arrived in 1948 remaining until 1971, and RMs came between 1963 and 1985 followed by RMLs in 1971. RFs were removed by 1971 with the arrival of the SMS and MBS classes. The LS eventually replaced these in 1978. DMSs first came here in 1973, and Metrobuses in 1981. When the garage closed on 20th July 1990, the Titan was the only type worked from here. Routes operated at April 1983 were 43, 134, 210 and W7.

The Sydney Road aspect of the garage at Muswell Hill in the early 1950s. Wire fencing has been erected along the pavement, although the reason for this is not clear. In 1954 the maximum run out was 91 buses, this had dropped to only 59 by the time of closure. (LTM)

The garage at Muswell Hill had a private road leading up from Hampden Road, and the buses in this view are parked alongside on vacant land. Park Royal bodied RT 776 is in the foreground, and was based here from December 1952 until January 1956. (Mick Webber Collection)

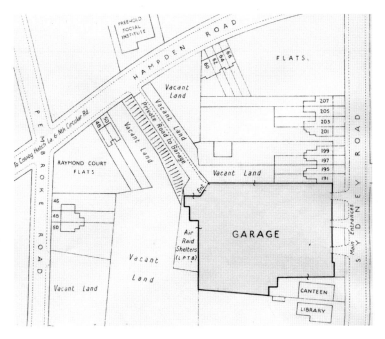

RM 248 came to Muswell Hill in 1982, and is fitted with one of the earlier bodies without upper deck front opening windows. This changed from RM 254 when quarter drop openers were fitted as standard. (Peter Horner)

NEW CROSS (NX)

New Cross tram depot was built by the LCC and opened in 1910, being London's largest and operating 258 trams in 1949. When the tram to bus conversions reached the final stage in July 1952, a complete rebuild was necessary, and in addition a completely new garage was to be built at Rye Lane to share the work. Officially, it became a bus garage on 6th July 1952, but the rebuilding work was far from complete, and operations were shared with other garages until it could take over on 12th November. RTs were the first to work here, including a few 2RT2s.

RFs came in 1958 from Old Kent Road when that garage closed, and in 1961, RMs made an appearance. A few RMLs came between 1975 and 1986. The RTs were finally removed in 1976. MBSs replaced RFs in 1968, and they in turn were replaced in 1972. The SMS arrived in 1970 and the DMS in 1972. The Metropolitan MD class made its debut in 1977, and then the Titan in 1983. The garage is still in operation. Routes operated at April 1983 were 1, 21, 37, 53, 70, 141, 171, 177, 184, 188, N82 and Inter Station.

The access to New Cross garage from Pepys Road in January 1967. The office and canteen building is on the left, and the garage on the right. The covered area could house over 200 buses, and the large forecourt provided plenty of space for other vehicles as well as staff cars. (Mick Webber)

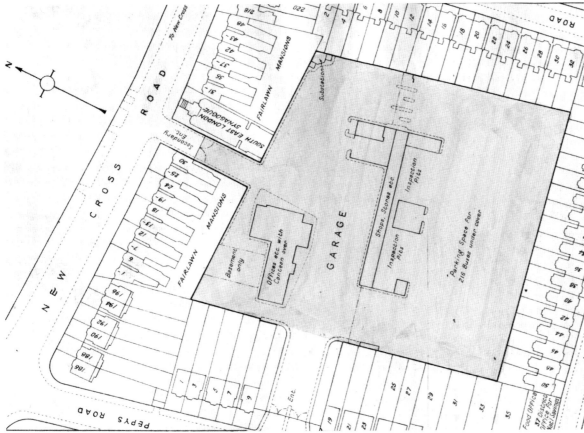

A September 1954 view inside New Cross. A huge area free of supports greatly aided bus manoeuvres here. The pit area is on the right, and the lines of RTs contain four 2RT2s still in service. (LTM)

January 1967. The entrance from New Cross Road, with the garage in front and the office and canteen block to the right. London Transport gully emptier 1040Q is on the left.

The eastern entrance to the garage area at New Cross. RF 388 and RT 4319 are parked in front of two RMs. Route 202A was a rush hour variant of the 202, and seven RFs were needed to work these duties. (Mick Webber)

Part of the garage forecourt at New Cross, looking toward the Pepys Road exit, the provision of which required the demolition of four of the terraced houses in this street.. The crew of RT 1337 are probably on a meal break, as it has just arrived in from route 1. It is January 1967. (Mick Webber)

RT 119 had been withdrawn from passenger service in March 1955, and remained in stock as a staff bus and trainer. It moved finally to New Cross in November 1962, and a visit on 14th September 1963 revealed its latest use as a turnover vehicle, seen here on its side on the forecourt. It was sold for scrap in that December. A new RM for the sightseeing tour is on the left. (Mick Webber)

NORBITON (NB)

The chronic overcrowding at Kingston was finally eased when a new garage was built at Norbiton, opening on 14th May 1952. Due to lack of space on the site, a main docking unit was created in a separate modernised building on the south side of London Road. The allocation of buses at Kingston halved overnight when many of their routes were transferred to the new garage. RT and T types were the initial allocation, and RFs and TDs followed. The Routemaster first came here in 1962 with the final stage of the trolleybus conversion scheme alterations. In 1971 the new one man buses arrived, with the SMS, DMS and BL classes. The RMs had gone by 1973, but returned in 1975 to take the place of the last RTs. Metrobuses worked from 1979. The garage was later closed on 7th September 1991, and subsequently demolished. Routes operated at April 1983 were 71, 72, 85, 131, 213A, 215, 216 and 218. A superstore was built on the site.

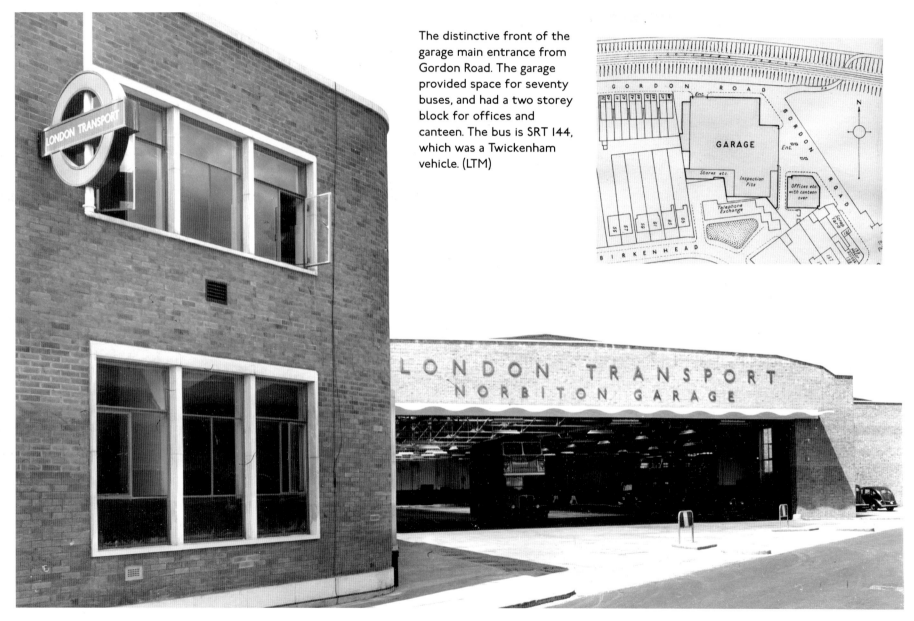

The distinctive front of the garage main entrance from Gordon Road. The garage provided space for seventy buses, and had a two storey block for offices and canteen. The bus is SRT 144, which was a Twickenham vehicle. (LTM)

The pit area at Norbiton is occupied by a Twickenham SRT in for maintenance. The facility was separate from the main building and had just opened in this view, with everything in pristine condition. Buses from Twickenham, Mortlake and Kingston were dealt with here. (LTM)

NORWOOD (N)

This LGOC garage was opened on 11th March 1909, and enlarged in 1925. ST and LT types were the main allocation in the pre-war years, with RTs arriving in 1950 and RMs in 1964. The RMs took over completely when the RTs left in 1970. The garage was closed on 24th April 1981 and demolished to make way for a completely new building. Work was transferred temporarily to the reopened Clapham garage. The new building was completed and opened on 27th October 1984 and remains in use. At April 1983, routes were operated by Clapham.

A panoramic view of the maintenance area at Norwood on 19th September 1936. LT and ST types were the sole allocation at this time, and LTs 707 and 349 can be seen on the left. On the right, being worked on are ST 298, LT 337, LT 1200 and LT 1176. ST 24 can just be seen on the far right. Routes 2, 3 and 68 operated from here in 1936. (LTM)

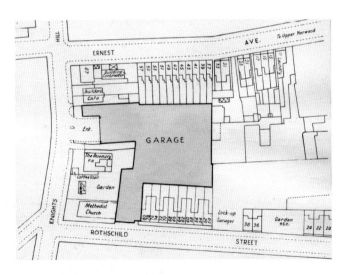

The front of Norwood garage facing Knights Hill in the mid-1960s. Two buses were supplied to work the summer only route 137A, and RT 2613 is blinded up to work this. RM 2082 is parked up ready for a journey on the 2B. (Peter Jones)

NUNHEAD (AH)

The garage at Nunhead was first opened in 1911 by the National Steam Car Company, but was closed on 18th November 1919. The LGOC reopened it on 21st April 1920. A large fleet of LTs worked from here in the mid-1930s, and after the war RTs arrived followed by a brief RTL allocation in 1951. In May 1950, for one week, RTWs were worked on the 12 in an experiment to prove the suitability of 8 feet wide buses on central routes. With new garages in the area being built,

Nunhead was found to be surplus to requirements, and was closed on 5th January 1954. The building was used afterwards for maintenance on the LT miscellaneous fleet, but was eventually sold. It has since been demolished and new housing built, although the clock tower remains in place. At time of closure, the maximum vehicle requirement was 90, and routes operated were 12, 37, 63 and 173.

The garage at Nunhead on Nunhead Lane in the mid-1930s. The vehicle run out remained at between 90 and 100 throughout the London Transport period, but new premises at nearby Peckham, Rye Lane, Walworth and Clapham meant it was no longer needed. (LTM)

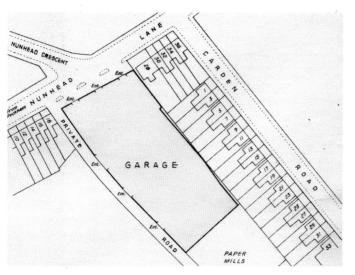

The pit area at Nunhead in 1936. The two buses being worked on nearest the camera are LTs 392 and 30. LT 392 seems to be getting most of the attention, and NS 70 on the far right also has men in attendance. (LTM)

It is 29th June 1935, and the busmen are on strike at Nunhead. This was probably a local dispute, as no London wide strike occurred at this time. (Topfoto)

OLD KENT ROAD (P)

A horse tram depot occupied this site from 1874, and after closure it was purchased by the Vanguard Motorbus Company, and converted into a bus garage. It later passed to the LGOC in 1908. In LT days, it was the last garage to operate open top NSs in August 1934, and it also housed the private hire fleet from 1937. The Inter Station Leyland Cubs were also stationed here from 1936, and STs and LTs formed the bulk of the service fleet. Single deck LTs and Qs also worked here, with RFs coming in 1952. RTs arrived in 1948, and remained the double deck allocation until closure on 25th November 1958. As late as 1950, a new canteen was built in Malt Street, a short walk away from the garage. Maximum vehicle requirement at closure was 81 and routes operated were 1, 4, 13, 17, 53, 78, 89A, 202 and Inter Station. The site has since been completely redeveloped, and a McDonalds built here.

Above: Old Kent Road garage from Bowles Road. The garage covered all of the ground behind the houses in the centre of this view, and had another entrance on the far left. Buses running in showed "Old Kent Road, Lord Wellington" on their blinds. (LTM)

Left: Old Kent Road garage on 15th May 1936. A good selection of buses in this view, comprising of NS 1080 on the far left, an unidentified NS and LT, and then two Leyland Lion Dodson bodied single-deckers LN 2 and LN 6, STL 404 and ST 464. The ST shows blinds for route 10, which had a lot of light running to gain access to the route. Six blue and cream STs were allocated for inter station duties between 1943 and 1946. (LTM)

The entrance at the end of Bowles Road with RF 459. The RFs were used on route 202. Some of the private hire fleet were still housed here, and an RFW can be seen inside the garage next to the RT. (Norman Rayfield)

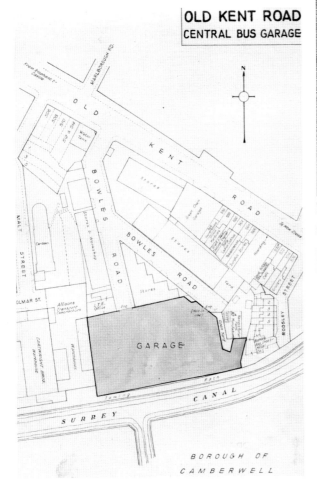

OLD KENT ROAD
CENTRAL BUS GARAGE

Route 89A commenced in January 1955 and was withdrawn in April 1958, and during that time Old Kent Road garage worked it on Saturdays only with four RTs, Catford supplying the Mon-Fri buses. RT 2354 is parked outside the garage, and would run light to Lewisham to take up route. RT 2354 demonstrates the use of experimental traffic indicators. (Norman Rayfield)

Palmers Green was another LGOC garage, and was opened on 27th July 1912. Most standard types worked here in the 1930s, ST, STL, NS and double and single deck LTs. After the war, in 1949 and 1950, SRTs, RTWs and RTLs came, although they were replaced by RTs in 1951. Routemasters made their debut in 1969, but the RTs hung on until 1978. The garage was modernised in the early 1970s, and a few RFs came in 1971. 1976 saw the SMS replace the RFs and the DMS class in turn replaced them in 1977. Metrobuses swept them aside in 1981. The garage remains open. Routes operated at April 1983 were 29, 34, 102 and 121.

The exterior of Palmers Green garage in Regents Avenue in 1967. Modernisation has since altered the appearance considerably. A memorial stone to the war dead can be seen on the left. (Mick Webber)

RT 2563 emerges from the garage to take up service on the 112 in March 1967. The 112 terminated here, and was shared with Stonebridge, who used RTLs on the route. (Mick Webber)

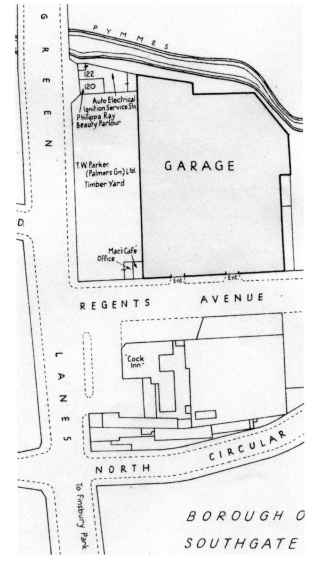

RT 2399 went to Palmers Green after overhaul in November 1969, and although it was delicensed four times during its spell there, it remained until April 1978 when it became a staff bus. This view was taken in January 1974 after the garage had been modernised. (Peter Horner)

Palmers Green garage on 16th July 1936. The two buses on the left are LTs 419 and 369, with NS 933 on the right. Other NSs on the right are being worked on. The roof here had to be raised after the war to allow RT family buses sufficient clearance. (LTM)

PECKHAM (PM)

Bull Yard in Peckham was originally owned by Thomas Tilling, who used it as a motor bus garage in 1904. When it passed to London Transport, it was used as a store for buses, and it was destroyed by enemy bombing in October 1940, many buses being written off, including all but one of the private hire TF coaches. A new garage was built and opened here on 2nd May 1951; it had a large forecourt which was used as a terminal point. In July 1952, it was home to some staff from nearby New Cross, whilst that depot was still being converted to a bus garage. RTs were the first vehicles to work here with some STLs officially allocated to New Cross. RMs came in 1963 with RMLs in 1971. Some XAs worked here for route P3 in 1970, although these were replaced by SMSs in 1973. The LS took over from the SMS in 1978. DMSs arrived in 1972 and the first Metropolitan type MD came in 1976, but was gone by 1982, when Routemasters took over the Central London routes. The garage was closed on 29th January 1994 and was demolished. A bus station now occupies the site. Work was transferred to New Cross and Camberwell. Routes operated at April 1983 were 12, 36, 36A, 36B, 63, 78, P3, P5, N85 and N86.

An early view of Peckham garage. The substantial building also housed the Medical Centre for London Transport South East which was in the section built over the main exit. The main block housed the traffic offices and conductors rooms on the ground floor, and the canteen and recreational facilities on the first floor. (LTM)

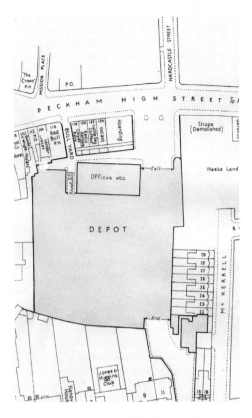

A view taken in May 1951 from the pit area. The Festival of Britain ran from May to October 1951, and special services were operated by London Transport to the South Bank. The STLs in this picture were assembled to work these routes, and seen here are STLs 404, 765, 845, 876, 690 and 868. (LTM)

Above: The pit area in July 1951. Newly delivered RT 2564 on the far left, stands next to RTs 444, 1664 and 3084. Extra pits were provided in the main garage that could be covered when not in use to provide extra space when needed. (LTM)

Left: This March 1967 scene shows RM 1441 with other RMs and RTs in a garage that was able to take 150 buses. The roof was of a concrete barrel vault construction in two sections separated by a cross beam, seen here on the right. (Mick Webber)

A mid-1950s view of RT 2590 trying out the new Essex bus washing machine. The Hanover Park entrance is on the right. (John Aldridge Collection)

PLUMSTEAD (AM)

The garage in Kings Highway Plumstead was opened by the LGOC on 15th October 1913. It was closed between 12th November 1914 and 19th November 1919, when it was requisitioned by the War Office. In the 1930s, LT type double-deckers dominated here, and there was a maximum requirement of 79 in 1937. After the war, RTLs arrived in 1949 but were exchanged for RTs in 1955, and they stayed until 1978. RMs came in 1967 for a three year period, and MBs were allocated in 1969. The DMS arrived in 1974, and they were replaced by the MDs in 1980. The expansion of nearby Thamesmead in the 1980s meant Abbey Wood and Plumstead were unable to cope with route demands, and they were both closed on 30th October 1981 and replaced by a new garage near to Plumstead Station (PD). The old garage was demolished and replaced by a superstore. Maximum vehicle requirement at closure was 49 and routes operated were 99, 122, 122A and 192.

Plumstead garage on 14th January 1937. LT 1237 is in the centre of a row of LTs in a period when this was the only type operated from here. Single deck LT 1142 on the left is a visiting bus. (LTM)

A view through the Wickham Lane door at Plumstead garage on 11th December 1966. RTs 1234, 1989 and 1773 face the camera. RT 1989 is a New Cross bus terminating here on the Sunday extension of route 53, which ran on from Plumstead Common to the garage, via Kings Highway, a road not served on any other day. (Mick Webber)

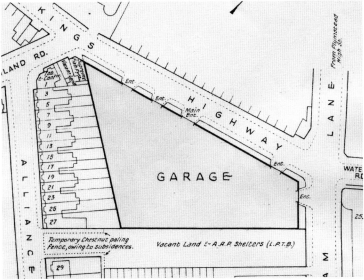

A 1967 view of Plumstead on the corner of Wickham Lane and Kings Highway. Post war discussions to enlarge the garage had come to nothing due to underground shaft discoveries which made the site unsuitable. (Mick Webber)

PLUMSTEAD (PD)

The new housing area at Thamesmead was rapidly expanding, and new bus services were needed. The existing bus garages at Abbey Wood and Plumstead were inadequate, and as a solution, a new premises was sought. A site near to Plumstead Station in the centre of a new road layout was identified, and the new garage was built, opening on

31st October 1981, with the two old garages closing the day before. The garage was big enough to house 135 buses, and had a large yard. The entire allocation was of the MD class Metropolitan, although these began to be replaced after a year by Titans. Routes operated at April 1983 were 99, 122, 161, 177, 178, 180, 198, 198A, 272 and 291.

Right: The new garage seen shortly after opening in 1981.

Below: The second day of operation at the new Plumstead garage. MDs 108, 142, 161, 16 and 13 can be seen. It must have been beneficial for the engineering staff to only have one type of bus to maintain. (Mick Webber)

POPLAR (PR)

The tram shed at Poplar was built by the LCC and opened in 1906. London Transport converted it to trolleybus operation in June 1940, in what was to be the final tram to trolleybus changeover. The trolleybus era here lasted until November 1959, when on the 11th, for the first time in the conversion programme, Routemasters were used for their intended purpose. The garage was huge and could house 194 buses, so it still had plenty of space after 58 RMs arrived. The closure of nearby Athol Street in May 1961 brought some RTLs, although these were replaced in 1968 by RTs with some new MBs for the 108. SMs followed on and then LSs in 1978. The DMS arrived in 1971 being replaced by Titans in 1982. The RTs here remained until 1976 and the Routemaster until 1984. The garage never realised its full potential, and it was closed on 2nd November 1985, work being transferred to West Ham, Clapton, Bow and Upton Park. The building still stands. Routes operated at April 1983 were 23, 40, 56, 108, 277, S2 and N84. The building still stands and is in use as a data security warehouse. The arched entrances neighbouring the road have been bricked up.

The large brick shed at Poplar was always under-used. It suffered some damage during the war, and was frequently used to store delicensed buses. Due to its closeness to the docks, QI trolleybuses were kept here prior to their sale to Spanish operators in 1961. (Gerald Mead)

RTLs first came to Poplar in 1961 when Athol Street closed, and remained a fixture until 1968. RTLs 1556, 424, 68 and 517 are lined up in this September 1967 scene. (Mick Webber)

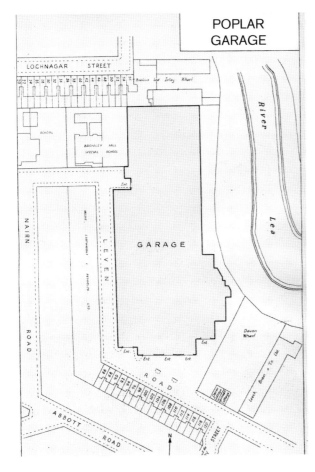

RM 1881 is the only double deck vehicle in this view, and has been out of service for some time judging by the state of the roof. It is 1976, and a programme of up-seating some SMS class vehicles, to be re-classified SMD, was to begin. Poplar was chosen as the venue for this work, because of the space available, and SMS 67, 70, 78 and 79 are seen here prior to work starting. (Capital Transport).

POTTERS BAR (PB)

Overground was a subsidiary of the LGOC, and a garage was built for them at Potters Bar, opening on 28th May 1930. By the late 1930s, the whole allocation here was of the ST class. Some open staircase LTs arrived during the war, and in 1947, its long association with the RT began. Routemasters came in 1964, and the RTs finally departed in 1971. A small allocation of RFs for the 284 arrived in 1968, but were ousted by MBs and later in 1971, SMSs. FRM 1 worked here in 1973 for a three year period. The DMS made an appearance in 1973, replacing the RMs. The Metrobus first came in 1981, and Routemasters returned briefly in 1982. It is the most northerly central bus garage, and is still in use. Routes operated at April 1983 were 242, 263, 298, 313 and PB1.

Potters Bar garage from the High Street in the mid-1930s. An ST is on the left-hand approach road, whilst Dennis DA10 occupies the exit road on the right. The well-manicured gardens make a pleasant scene complete, although this area is now all given up to car parking. (LTM)

A 1950 view of the garage interior. A lone STL 574 can be seen by the back wall, together with RTs 217, 208, 939, 437 and 936. Restricted blind displays were still the order of the day. (LTM)

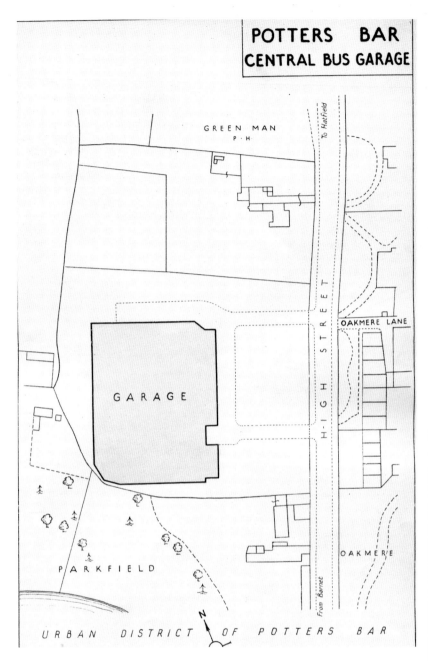

POTTERS BAR
CENTRAL BUS GARAGE

GREEN MAN
P·H·

To Hatfield

OAKMERE LANE

H I G H   S T R E E T

GARAGE

From Barnet

OAKMERE

PARKFIELD

URBAN   DISTRICT   OF   POTTERS   BAR

RT 2449 had been at Potters Bar since September 1969, and would move on to Hounslow in July 1971. This was taken in May 1971, with the bus sandwiched between an RM and an SMS. (Peter Horner)

RT 4343 left Aldenham after overhaul and went to Potters Bar, but by August it had moved on to Palmers Green. It is seen here in that short period at PB with RT 4437 at the rear. (Denis Battams)

A nice scenic view of Potters Bar during the RT period in the 1960s with RT 4259 on the left. The gardens are still being tended at this point, before being given over to tarmac. (Michael Rouum)

PUTNEY, CHELVERTON ROAD (AF)

This site of horse stables was built and opened as a bus garage by the LGOC on 18th July 1912. In London Transport days, it was the last garage to operate solid tyred buses, when the NS type was replaced in July 1935. When rebuilding work was carried out in 1935/6, buses on route 30 were operated by the ex-tram depot at Chiswick. STLs were the main allocation in the late thirties, and it was here that RT1 made its first appearance, the "pre-war" class being shared with its neighbour, Putney Bridge. Some RTWs arrived here for a week in May 1950 to take part in suitability trials of 8 feet wide buses in central London, working on the 28. A proper RTW allocation came in 1952 and in 1955 the RTs were replaced by RTLs. The Leylands were all replaced later by RTs which were here until 1970. The first RMs arrived in 1962 and RMLs in 1965. The year 1971 saw the SMS and later the DMS move in, and the Metrobus replaced these in 1983. Routes operated at April 1983 were 14, 30, 74, 85 and 164. The garage remains open.

A photograph taken just after the garage was modernised in 1936. It is tucked away in a back street, and behind the rather modest entrance a large space opens up to accommodate nearly 100 buses. The two buses here are STLs 1249 and 1139. STL 1249 was the only bus to bear the "BLT" registration mark. (LTM)

A view of the pit area at Chelverton Road on 23rd September 1936. The buses are STLs 1406, 1216, 1596, 1192 and 1346. STL 1216 and 1596 have just been delivered new. A run out of just over 80 buses was needed in this period. The garage sweeper is seen on the left. (LTM)

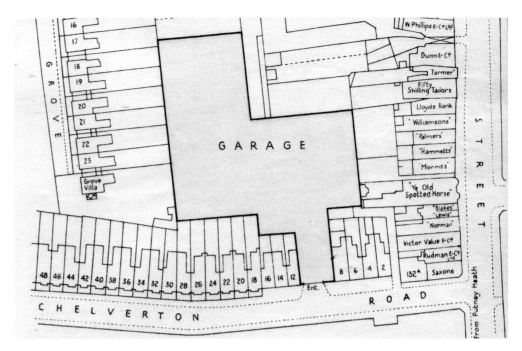

This garage was opened in 1913 by the National Steam Car Company. It was closed in 1919, but re-opened by the LGOC on 21st January 1920. STLs were the main allocation in the late 1930s, and later the first RTs worked from here and Chelverton Road in 1939, over 60 of the type being allocated here. After the war, in 1949, RTWs came, and in June 1950, some were used on the central London trials of the type on route 14. A few post war RTs also arrived, but all were replaced in 1955 by RTLs. They remained in charge until closure on 26th November 1958. Maximum vehicle requirement at closure was 75 and routes operated were 14, 74, 85, 93 and 96. The building was later demolished.

The rather attractive front of Putney Bridge garage facing west on the High Street. The northern wall of the garage bordered the Thames. RTL 1075 on the right only came to the garage in August 1958, but unlike most of the buses here, it went to Turnham Green unlicensed, before finding further service at Mortlake in December. (Norman Rayfield)

The rear door at Putney Bridge opened on to Brewhouse Street, and beyond the end wall is the River Thames. Access to Putney Bridge Road could be gained from here. (John Gillham)

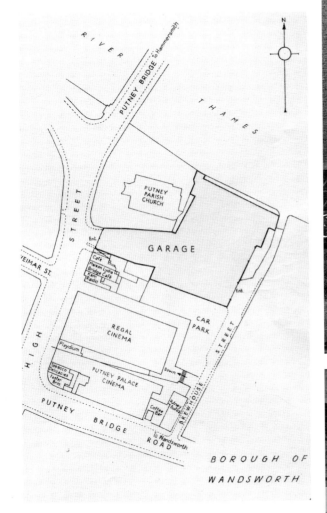

STL 1119 is over the pit at Putney Bridge on 12th May 1938, and two of the staff are operating machinery to the left. White summer coats were perhaps not too practical for this kind of work! (LTM)

RIVERSIDE (R)

Bradmore House occupied this site, and when the LGOC built its bus garage here, opening on 8th December 1913, it retained the original frontages in Queen Caroline Street and Great Church Lane as access points to the new garage. The first K and NS type buses were operated from here. The garage was known as Hammersmith until renamed Riverside in 1950 to avoid confusion with nearby Hammersmith trolleybus depot. In the late 1930s, LT types worked from here with an allocation of over ninety. The first post-war buses here were RTLs in 1949 and RTWs in 1950. Some of the RTWs took part in suitability trials in May 1950 of 8 feet wide vehicles in central London, on routes 17, 27A and 88. These remained until the RTLs (1965) and RTWs (1966) were replaced by RTs. RMs arrived in 1966, and RMLs in 1967. Some RFs came in 1970 for the 290, but gave way to BLs in 1976. RMLs left in 1978, and the standard Routemaster remained until closure on 24th June 1983. During the 1960s a Green Line RF was kept here to cover for central London breakdowns. Routes operated at April 1983 were 11, 27, 73. Bradmore House has now been restored and the building is now in use as a restaurant.

Above right: Mortlake LT 966 leaves Riverside garage by way of the Great Church Lane door in the late 1940s. The bus was withdrawn in January 1950. Route 73 was shared between Mortlake and Tottenham and required 90 buses on Mon-Fri operation. (Fred Ivey)

Right: The Great Church Lane access in July 1959 which incorporated the Hammersmith underground entrance. The trolleybus wires are in place, but would be redundant the following year. This building has since been demolished. (John Gillham)

124

RM 1618 is a Tottenham bus that has terminated at Riverside on route 73. An inspector stands by, no doubt to supervise proceedings. (Peter Horner)

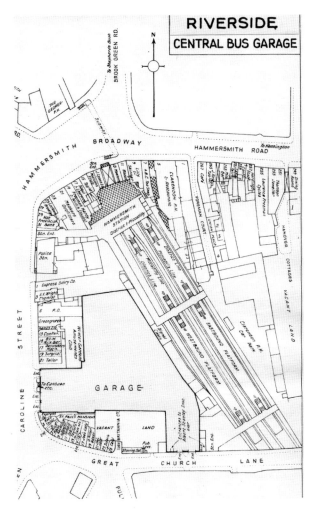

Riverside Routemasters 330 and 1902 rest by the bus washer in the early 1980s. Riverside had a maximum of 15 RMs for route 73 in the Mon-Fri rush hour. (Peter Horner)

NORTH STREET, ROMFORD (NS)

The new garage at Romford was built on land formally used as allotments. It opened on 12th August 1953, and provided room for 115 buses, although only 67 began operations on the first day, the types being STLs, RTLs, SRTs and TDs. RTs soon arrived at the end of the year, and gradually the other double deck types were replaced by the end of the following year. RFs took over from the TDs in 1959. RMs were allocated in 1966 and SMS class buses came in 1971, although they were superseded by the DMS from 1972. The first London BLs worked here in 1976, and the LSs in 1980. Some of the front entrance Routemaster RMA type worked from here on the 175 in 1975 and 1976. RTs left in 1977 and DMSs in 1980, when new Titans arrived. The Titan also saw off the last RMs in 1982. It remains operational. Routes operated at April 1983 were 66, 66A, 103, 174, 175, 193, 247, 294, 296 and N98.

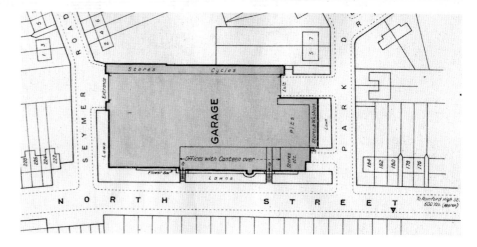

A dramatic sky over the new garage at North Street Romford in August 1953. The entrance was by way of Seymour Road, to the left of this view, with exit on to Park Drive on the right. The canteen and offices are in the centre section with a stores building to the right. (LTM)

The main shed at North Street in March 1967 looking towards the Seymour Road entrance. RM 1877 is on the left next to RT 3168, and RTs 3065, 1564 and 3943 are in view. The main garage administrative buildings are to the left. (Mick Webber)

RYE LANE (RL)

This site has long been associated with London's transport. In 1872, it was a horse tram depot, and was used by the LCC between 1904 and 1906, before becoming a workshop, and then in London Transport days, a permanent way depot. The site was cleared and as part of the tramway replacement programme, a new bus garage was built and opened on 6th January 1952. Eighty new RTs moved in to operate new routes 69, 149, 178 and 179. It worked some routes on behalf of New Cross and Stockwell whilst their building work was completed. Routemasters joined the allocation in 1962, and there was a brief interlude of RTLs in 1964/5, but it was RTs and RMs that were there when the garage closed on 22nd March 1969. Maximum vehicle allocation at closure was 88, and routes operated were 12, 13, 36A, 36B, 37, 173 and N85. Work was transferred to Peckham and Camberwell. The site is now occupied by a supermarket and car park.

The garage entrance was in Bellenden Road with the canteen and offices in the building on the left. In LT's pre-war plans for the south London tram replacement, this was intended to be a trolleybus depot until the war intervened, and tram replacement plans changed to buses instead. (Norman Rayfield)

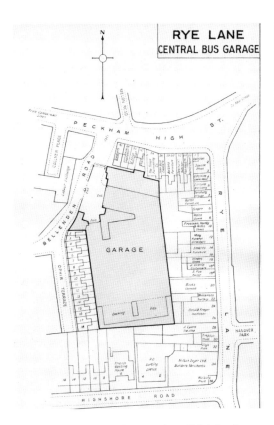

RYE LANE
CENTRAL BUS GARAGE

Rye Lane garage in September 1954, looking towards the pit area. The garage was designed to house 115 buses, and although this capacity was never met, it came close in late 1952 with 108 RTs being allocated. (LTM)

SEVEN KINGS (AP)

This LGOC garage opened on 8th May 1913. In London Transport days in 1937, it had a large contingent of the LT class, but after the war, the new RTs appeared in 1948, only to be replaced in 1949 by RTLs. A few RTWs arrived in 1950 for about a year. RTs returned in 1958 to take over from the RTLs, and they were the only allocation here until 1976 when some RMs came, and eventually by 1977, the RTs had left. The DMS made an appearance in 1976, but they too had left by 1980 when the Titans began to arrive. The garage was substantially rebuilt and modernised in 1976, but the loss of tendered routes led to its closure on 19th March 1993. Routes operated at April 1983 were 86, 129, 139, 148, 150 and 225.

The front of Seven Kings garage on the High Road. The LGOC stone plaque showing the year 1913 can be seen at the top of the building. This traditional frontage was to be completely demolished during the 1976 rebuilding. (Robin Newell)

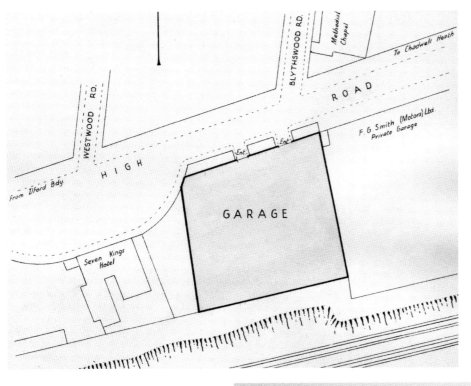

Top right: RT 3225 at Seven Kings garage in February 1976. The building work is well underway, and soon the garage will be transformed. It was the last garage to have an all RT allocation, which it relinquished in 1976 after nearly twenty years. (Peter Horner)

Right: The new Seven Kings garage building on the main High Road in about 1981. Much of the original shed at the rear remains. (Gerald Mead)

SHEPHERDS BUSH (S)

This garage was originally opened on 17th February 1907 by the London Motor Omnibus Company, and passed to the LGOC in 1908. It was closed during the First War on 1st November 1914, and didn't reopen until 14th July 1923. In 1937 it had an all LT allocation on the 12, 88 and 105 routes. The post-war period saw RTLs arrive in 1949, followed by RTWs. Some of the RTWs were used for the central London suitability trials in May 1950. They were the only types here until 1960. The main building was demolished, completely rebuilt and enlarged in 1954. When the trolleybus depot at Hammersmith closed in 1960, Shepherds Bush played a major role in the replacement programme, RMs being drafted in. RTWs left in 1961, and the RTLs were replaced by RTs in 1965. The DMS first worked here in 1971, and stayed until Metrobuses came in 1983. The RT allocation ceased in 1978, and the RML joined the RMs in 1975. The garage is still in operation. Routes operated at April 1983 were 72, 88, 220 and 283.

Shepherds Bush garage before and after rebuilding in 1954. In the top view STLs 1178 and 934 can be seen inside the garage, whilst on the right is LT 283 and STL 1210. The garage doors still bear the LGOC ownership in this mid-1930s view. The sparkling new garage, below, just after opening in 1954. Wells Road is in the foreground, and the office and canteen block is in the background on the right. Terminated buses used the area in front of the canteen. (LTM)

A view inside Shepherds Bush in December 1961 showing trainer RM 298, RT 34 and RM 366. The RT was working as a trainer from Chalk Farm on 23rd November, when it struck a low bridge in Latchmere Road, Clapham. RM 366 is blinded up for the 220, which replaced trolleybus route 630 the previous year. (Terry Cooper Collection/ Mick Webber)

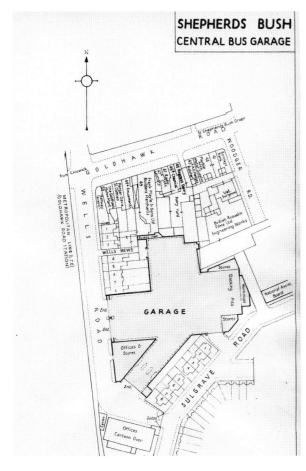

RTL 128 is a Riverside bus just back from its March 1964 overhaul, and is parked in the garage at Shepherds Bush. The main structure is of reinforced concrete, due to the shortage of steel at the time. The main pit area is in the background to the right. (Fred Ivey)

SIDCUP (SP)

The garage in Foots Cray High Street was opened on 11th June 1924 by the LGOC. In the mid-1930s, it operated single and double deck LTs, and after the war, it was the first garage to operate the production RTLs in December 1948. Single deck Q and T types worked here in the early post-war years, and for a brief spell a few SRTs worked in 1951. The Ts and Qs were replaced by the RF in 1951, and they stayed until 1958. The RTLs were swapped for RTs in 1955. New one man buses of the MB and later SMS class came in 1968 and 1973, and Routemasters in 1975. The SMSs left in 1976 when the DMS arrived. The Titan and Metrobus were allocated in 1982 for comparison trails, and later that year the Titans arrived in large numbers ousting the DMS. The garage was modernised in 1972, and the open area at the rear was enlarged. When the garage at Bexleyheath was reopened, Sidcup became surplus to requirements, and it was closed on 15th January 1988. Routes operated at April 1983 were 21, 21A, 51, 161, 228 and 229.

Foots Cray Road is very quiet in this 1930s picture of Sidcup garage. LT 690 is poised to emerge on route 21 to Wood Green. Sidcup would use 39 buses on this route on Mon-Fri, and 3 STs would be supplied from West Green. (LTM)

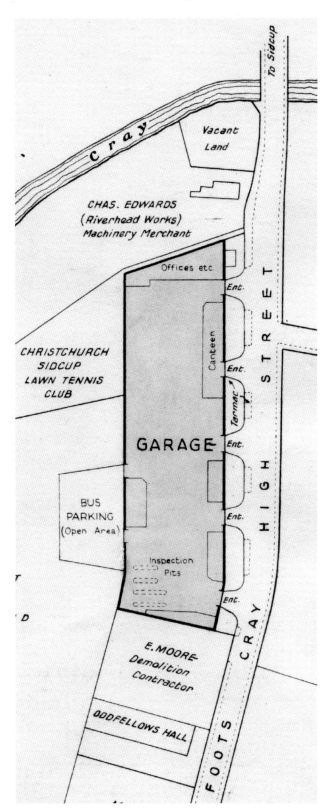

Above: Sidcup garage on 19th June 1974, and RT 3490 is on the left with distant RT 2517 on the right. The recently enlarged parking area can be seen through the door on the left, as two members of staff pass the time of day by the bus wash. (LTM)

Below: RMs 288, 493 and 572 are seen here in this view taken on 5th June 1982. Sidcup had a maximum Routemaster requirement of 35 buses in the peak hours at this time. (Peter Horner)

SOUTHALL (HW)

This former LGOC garage opened on 18th March 1925 as Hanwell, and was the first to operate the new ST class. Leyland TD class double-deckers taken over from independent companies, were based here in the period between 1933 and 1939, and the first RT chassis fitted with an old Dodson body and numbered ST1140, was tried out here in 1938. The utility Bristol buses B1-29 were all allocated here in 1942. STDs also worked for a while before being transferred to Loughton. Single-deck TDs came in 1948, being replaced by Ts in 1952, and they in turn replaced by RFs in 1958. The garage was renamed Southall in 1950 to avoid confusion with nearby Hanwell trolleybus depot. The RTL and RTW classes appeared in 1949, but only lasted until 1951 when RTs took over and stayed until 1978. In 1968 the RML and MB classes were allocated, but the RMLs left in 1971 when some SMSs came, followed by the DMS in 1973. Standard Routemasters and SMs arrived in 1978, and the Metrobus replaced the DMS in 1979. The garage was all Metrobus from 1982, and was closed on 8th August 1986. Routes operated at April 1983 were 92, 105, 120, 195, 232, 273, 274 and 282.

The garage was extended in 1931, and the two separate buildings can be seen in this pre-war view with STL 1369 parked in the doorway. The trams passing here would be replaced by trolleybuses in November 1936, and the new trolleybus traction standards are in place together with some of the wiring. (LTM)

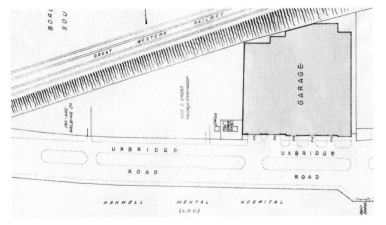

Southall was the last garage that RT 3986 worked as a service bus between January 1977 and April 1978. RTs will soon depart from this garage, the immediate future being in the hands of the DMS. (Norman Rayfield)

STAMFORD BROOK (V)

Few central bus garages have had a more varied career than Stamford Brook. It started life as Chiswick tram depot, a horse car shed that was converted to electric cars by the London United Tramways in 1901. It was bought by the LCC in 1922, and passed to London Transport who used it as a store for surplus trams. When London Transport commenced its tram to trolleybus conversions at Hammersmith depot, building work restricted space for the new vehicles, and therefore Chiswick was used operationally for some 626, 628 and 630 trolleybuses from September 1937 for a few months. Buses were operated on route 30 from here between July 1935 and February 1936 whilst building work was underway at Chelverton Road garage. During a meeting of the Engineering Committee in April 1934, it was proposed that Chiswick tram depot be demolished and rebuilt as a bus garage to replace Shepherds Bush and Turnham Green. This proposal was subsequently rejected. During the war some repairs and war damage work was carried out here on both buses and trolleybuses. After the war, many trolleybuses were worked on here, including 82, that had their staircases rebuilt. In 1966, the BEA coaches that were operated by London Transport of behalf of the airline, were moved here from Hammersmith, and stayed until 1978. The signwriting on the Silver Jubilee Routemasters was carried out here in 1977. Work to modernise the building commenced in 1978, and it was ready in 1980, opening on 10th May as a replacement for Turnham Green that had closed the night before, its fleet of RMs, Ms and LSs being transferred. Routes operated at April 1983 were 27, 91, 237, 267, A1, A2, A3, E3 and N97.

The elegant arched front of the former tram depot at Stamford Brook with Metrobuses in evidence. Over £2 million was spent modernising the site including a new office and canteen block, and widened access. (Gerald Mead)

RMs 1906 and 1848 were renumbered SRM 18 and 2 for the fleet of silver Routemasters to celebrate the Queen's Silver Jubilee in 1977. The signwriting work was carried out at Stamford Brook, and the buses are seen here on the garage forecourt posing for the camera. (Capital Transport)

STAMFORD HILL (SF)

The tram shed at Stamford Hill was opened by the LCC in 1907, and London Transport converted it to trolleybus operation in 1939. The trolleybus reign came to an end in July 1961, when new Routemasters took over. Between 1965 and 1970, new XA Atlantean, XF Fleetlines and RMLs took part in evaluation trials here, with the RMLs leaving in 1966, and the others in 1969/70. The RML returned in 1970. New DMSs appeared in 1971 and DMs in 1974, although the DM was replaced in 1980 by newly repainted RCLs which had been returned to LT stock from London Country. These remained until 1984. The RMLs left again in 1981 only to re-appear in 1986, and in the meantime, Metrobuses came in 1982. The garage closed briefly in 1995 until 1996, and then closed again between 2000 and 2002. It remains open. Routes operated at April 1983 were 67, 149, 243, 253 and N83.

RM 1743 follows a sister vehicle out of Stamford Hill to take up duty on route 253 in 1980. The tramway heritage of the building is apparent in this view. The routes still operated at this time retain the tram and trolleybus history with tram routes 49, 43 and 53, becoming trolleybus routes 649, 643 and 653, followed by bus routes 149, 243 and 253. (Terry Cooper Collection/Mick Webber)

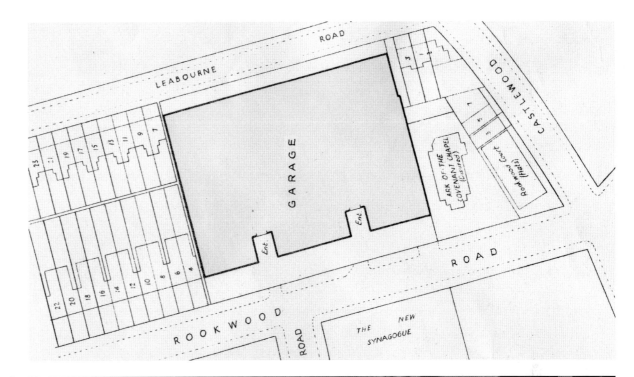

This 1980s view shows RMs 1164 and 694 with eight others. The garage remains very much the same as it was in the trolleybus era. (Terry Cooper Collection/Mick Webber)

STOCKWELL (SW)

The new garage at Stockwell was originally intended to operate trolleybuses in the tram to trolleybus conversions, but after the war it was decided that buses were the preferred option for tramway replacement. The garage that was designed here was to be unique, and was formed of nine concrete arches which gave the building a completely uninterrupted floor space, and an area that could accommodate 200 buses. The garage opened on 2nd April 1952 with a small allocation of RTLs for route 178. A few STLs also came to work the Festival Gardens service. The building work carried on into 1953, and the fleet of RTLs gradually built up as more routes were transferred in. A small number of post-war STDs arrived here during this period. After Clapham closed, more RTLs were drafted in, and the garage then had 160 buses allocated. In December 1962 the RM arrived to replace RTLs on the 37, and by 1966 the RML had joined the fleet, and the RTLs were shortly to be swapped for RTs. The garage provided buses for the Round London Sightseeing tour from 1970, and from 1973 new DMSs started to appear. The unsuccessful Shoplinker red and yellow Routemaster service also worked from here in 1979. The garage remains in use. Routes operated at April 1983 were 2, 2B, 44, 77A, 88, 170, P4, N68, N81 and N87.

The garage at Stockwell from Lansdowne Way. RTL 1266 is dwarfed by the large structure, which is now a listed building. Route 178 was the first to work here when 12 buses were transferred in from Rye Lane. (LTM)

It is 10pm on 23rd March 1967, and many of the buses have finished for the day. RM, RML and RTL classes are all in view, and the wet garage floor suggests a rotten night. Sadly, the arched fluorescent lights have all now been replaced by more sensible fittings. (Mick Webber)

RTs 4638 and 1808 form the end of two line-ups at Stockwell on 15th October 1967. The graceful arches here cannot fail to impress in an area where 100 buses look lost! These two buses were destined to stay here for another two and three years respectively. (Mick Webber)

Inside Stockwell in 1960 we see at the back of the garage a row of withdrawn 2RT2s and the overseas demonstration bus RTL 3. It will never have operated on route 24, shown on the blind, as it had been converted to offside staircase layout in 1958 to show potential buyers abroad the possibility of using RT family buses beyond the British Isles. RTL 3 was sold to a customer in Geneva in May 1964. (Denis Battams)

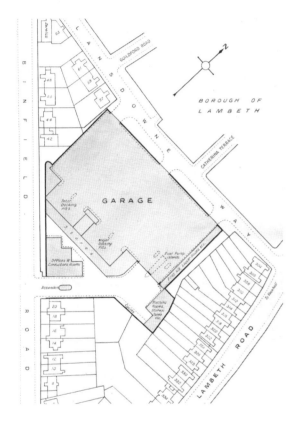

It is October 1967, and RTs are lined up next to an ambulance of the LT Corps of the St Johns Ambulance Brigade. The skylights and end arched glass panels ensure that plenty of natural light is available. (Mick Webber)

STONEBRIDGE (SE)

The Metropolitan Electric Tramways built and opened their depot at Stonebridge Park in 1906. It was a typical shed design, and similar to those at Finchley and Hendon. London Transport converted it to trolleybus operation in 1936, and when the trolleybus abandonment came in January 1962, it became a bus garage with an allocation of new Routemasters, and some RTLs. RTs replaced the RTLs in 1968, and these in turn were superseded by the SMS in 1971. Their tenure only lasted until 1976, when the DMS arrived. RMLs worked here between 1975 and 1979, when DMs took over. The Metrobus was the last standard type here arriving in 1980. The British Airways fleet was transferred here in 1978 until their withdrawal in 1979, and the space at the rear and side has often been used to store withdrawn buses. For some time the turnover vehicle 1036TV was based here, allowing breakdown crews to practice on lifting overturned vehicles. The garage was closed in 15th August 1981 and work transferred to Westbourne Park. The building still stands, and is in use as industrial units. Maximum vehicle requirement at closure was 40 and routes operated were 18, 112, 187, 260 and 266.

Stonebridge garage in 1980, and the new order is represented by two Metrobuses. Routemasters lurk in the background in front of the railway embankment. Note the memorial to the war dead on the left in front of the office block. (LTM)

The turnover bus was kept at Stonebridge for a few years, and when RT 106, known as 1036TV, was retired, Metro-Cammell bodied RTL 986 was used. It is pictured here on the waste ground next to the Harrow Road. (Mick Webber)

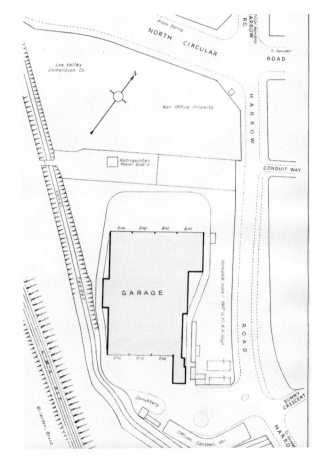

The forecourt at Stonebridge in 1978, and RMLs 881 and 2387 stand next to RMs 1123 and 1086. The two RMLs have the new number plate position modification, whilst the RMs retain the original style. (Peter Horner)

STREATHAM (AK)

This former LGOC garage was opened on 26th June 1913. In pre-war LT days its main allocation was of ST and LT types, with the STL coming later, but after the war, the RT dominated from 1950 to 1970, when RMs arrived. The RTs left in 1975. SMS class buses came in 1971 and were replaced in 1976 by the DMS. A lot of internal reconstruction took place in the 1960s, but the garage closed in 1984 for complete rebuilding. It reopened in 1987, but closed for good on 13th March 1992, initially becoming an indoor go-kart track. It is now a leisure centre. Routes operated at April 1983 were 49, 159 and 249.

It is 1953 and the Coronation is approaching. There is a board outside Streatham garage advertising Coronation tours, and a sticker on the bus stop is advising the public of bus excursions that are available from here. (LTM)

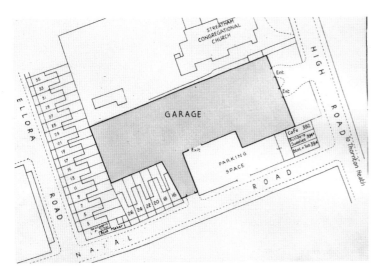

Streatham garage on 29th April 1967, and RTs 1901 and 1300 sit on the forecourt ready for service. It looks as though a fresh coat of white paint has been applied to the area around the doorway, and gardens were still in evidence to brighten the High Road. (Mick Webber)

SUTTON (A)

This ex LGOC garage was opened on 9th January 1924. In the mid-1930s, the STL and single deck LT were the main classes operated, but in 1946 the utility Daimlers started to arrive, and 100 worked here until replaced by RTLs in 1952. Three Maidstone Corporation Daimlers were allocated here whilst on loan in 1949/50. The RTLs were replaced by RTs in 1953/4, and the single deck LTs on route 213 were displaced by RFs in 1952. The RT remained in charge until 1976, when the DMS took over, having first arrived in the early 1970s. Routemasters came in 1976 but only stayed until 1982. The BL made its debut in 1976 and replaced the RFs. The garage is still in operation. Routes operated at April 1983 were 80, 93, 154, 164, 213A, 280 and 293.

RTL 1357 was new when it arrived at Sutton in December 1952. It was one of many that worked here until replaced by RTs in 1954, this one moving on to Walworth in January of that year. Two of a maximum of 21 RFs needed for the 213 can be seen in the background. (Alan Cross)

RT 4623 waits in the doorway on route 213 on 29th April 1967, and as with many garages, the garage wall provides a convenient parking area for staff vehicles. The bus stop flag on the wall seems like an afterthought. The 213 had been a single deck route until 1963. (Mick Webber)

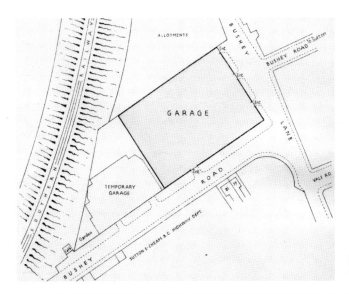

In October 1940, a bomb went through the roof at Sutton, and created the crater seen here. The clean-up is underway, and buses ran out as normal. No vehicles were lost in this incident. (LTM)

THORNTON HEATH (TH)

The tram shed on this site had been in use since 1879, and eventually was acquired by Croydon Corporation as an electric car shed in 1901. London Transport continued to operate trams from here until it was closed on 31st December 1949, its cars being transferred to nearby Purley depot. The shed was then demolished to enable a new garage to be built for the forthcoming tram to bus conversion. Although it was not complete, buses started working from here on 8th April 1951, with 54

new RTs on tram replacement routes. No other classes were operated until the RM arrived in 1962, the RTs finally departing in 1976. DMSs replaced the RMs in 1971, but returned in 1976 only to leave again in 1978. Their final appearance was in 1982, when they made their third visit. The SMS came in 1970 and left in 1980, and the DM arrived in 1978. Routes operated at April 1983 were 60, 64, 109, 157 and 194B. The garage remains operational.

The garage at Thornton Heath has not been open very long, and Brixton RT 3266 is in the middle doorway ready for the 109 after having turned short here. The garage was built to accommodate just over 100 buses, but never actually reached that level. (LTM)

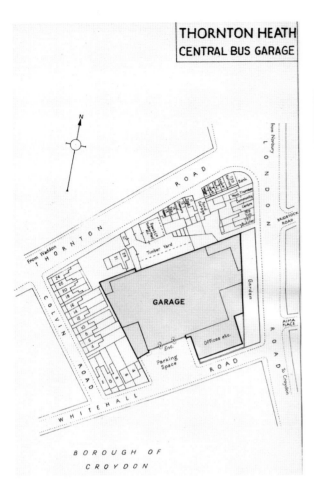

THORNTON HEATH
CENTRAL BUS GARAGE

GARAGE

BOROUGH OF
CROYDON

Two views of Thornton Heath whilst still under construction. In the top view RT 1889 is the only identifiable bus in a batch parked just inside the unfinished structure, and in the picture below, RTs 1889 and 1854 are parked amongst the builders materials blinded up for the 109. All of these buses came second-hand from Wandsworth.

TOTTENHAM (AR)

This garage was opened by the LGOC on 7th July 1913. It was closed during the first war between 2nd November 1914 and 25th June 1919. London Transport operated STL and both single and double deck LTs during the mid-1930s, and during the second war, it was allocated some utility Guys in 1942. RTLs and RTWs arrived in 1949, route 41 being the first to be worked by the RTW class, and TDs came to operate the 236 until RFs replaced them in 1958. RMs started to arrive in 1962 and the RTWs departed in 1964, the Routemasters staying until 1987. RTLs lasted until 1968. The RML and XA classes were used on evaluation trials in 1965/6, and FRM 1 first entered service here on route 76 in 1967. The DMS first came to Tottenham in 1972 for a ten year stay, after which the Metrobus took over their work. The garage remains in use. Routes operated at April 1983 were 41, 67, 73, 76, 171, 243, 243A, 259 and N90.

The aspect of Tottenham garage from Philip Lane in the 1930s. The front of the garage has since been partially rebuilt, but the "Caution Motor buses" sign on the far right is still in place. An allocation of 152 buses was required in the early 1950s. (LTM)

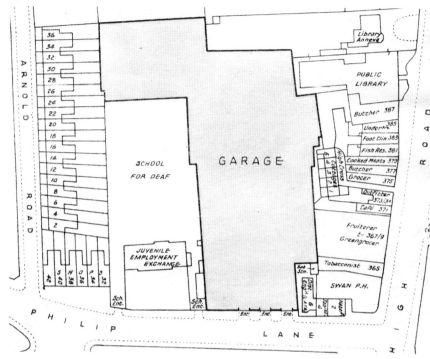

RM 596 stands alone in the middle of the garage ready for route 171. The recently allocated Metrobuses are in evidence in the early 1980s view. (Peter Horner)

Tottenham on 14th August 1976. A typical view of an RT in its final days. RT 2964 had arrived at Tottenham in March 1976, and by the end of August it had been delicensed and sold for scrap. It has an RM side blind as a front display here for route 41, and a rather oversized painted garage code. (Peter Horner)

TURNHAM GREEN (V)

Turnham Green garage was built on the site of horse bus stables, and opened on 8th May 1911. Because of its close proximity to Chiswick Works, it was often used as a first allocation for prototype and experimental buses. In LT days the first RTL numbered 501, and RM2 first worked from here, and the Chiswick skid bus was maintained here. For a while in the 1930s, the entire stock was of the ST class. The roof had to be raised in 1948 to accommodate the new RTs which arrived that year, and also some RTLs which only stayed until 1951. The RT was the main allocation until 1965 when some RMs were drafted in. The RT stayed until 1971. MBSs came in 1968, and the RMs left briefly until returning in 1970, but in 1971 the DMS made an appearance with some of the SMS class. The LS class replaced the SMS in 1978, and the Metrobus took over from the DMS in 1979. The garage closed on 9th May 1980, its work being transferred to Stamford Brook. Routes operated at closure were 27, 91, 237, 267, E3 and N97.

Turnham Green garage from Belmont Road. The garage occupied a triangular site in front of the embankment supporting the District line, and being surrounded by housing, there was no room for expansion. (Mick Webber)

RT 4345 from Hounslow swings in to Turnham Green garage on route 116, terminating before returning to Staines. The driver is using the entrance at the far end of Belmont Road. (Mick Webber)

A nice line up at Turnham Green in April 1980, just before closure. Home buses RMs 2206 and 598 stand next to Hounslow RM 1025, which has turned short on the 237. Metrobuses are also in evidence. (Peter Horner)

TWICKENHAM (AB)

Twickenham garage was opened on 30th March 1912 by the LGOC. It was used by the Royal Flying Corps between 19th January 1918 and 4th June 1919, and was also used to build bus bodies between 3rd May 1921 and 16th April 1924. Its fleet of STLs were employed on the 27a and 37 in the mid-1930s. After the second war some SRTs arrived in 1949, but were gradually replaced by RTs in 1950, a class that was to stay until closure. Some RTWs were drafted in for a week in May 1950 to work route 27A, in an experiment to prove to the police that the new 8 feet wide buses were suitable for central London routes. RFs came in 1968 for route 290. Twickenham was one of very few garages never to receive Routemasters. Buses running in showed "Richmond Bridge" on their blinds. Closure came on 18th April 1970, although the premises was later used by the Routemaster Heritage Trust for preserved buses. It has since been demolished. Routes operated at closure were 27A, 90, 90B and 290.

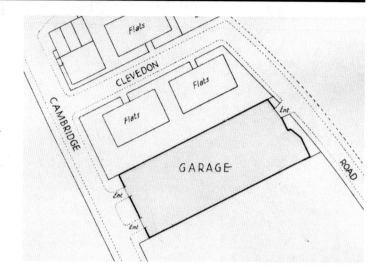

Looking like an oversized garden shed, Twickenham garage was overshadowed by a large oak tree, and tucked away in a quiet side street off of Richmond Road. Work moved to Fulwell and Riverside garage after closure. This view was taken in 1967. (Mick Webber)

The garage as seen from Cambridge Road showing RTs 2597, 3763, 1385 and 2224. Note the sign on the right hand door for Rover tickets, directing the public into the garage. To the left of the first bus was a small door leading to Clevedon Road, beyond which was the River Thames. (John Gillham)

UPTON PARK (U)

The London Road Car Company built the large garage at Upton Park, and it opened on 12th August 1907, passing to the LGOC the following year. Like many others, it closed in the first war between 3rd November 1915 and 28th May 1919. It was enlarged in 1931 to accommodate over 200 buses, and from 1934 until 1939 it operated many of the acquired Leyland double deck TD class together with NS, LT and STL types. Utility Guys also worked from here. The post-war RT arrived in 1948 and was joined by some RTWs in 1950. These classes remained until 1964 and 1976 respectively. RTLs also made occasional appearances during this period. RMs first arrived in 1964 and RMLs in 1966, and they stayed until 1982 and 1987. Modern one man buses came, the SMS in 1971, the DMS in 1973 and the Titan in 1981. The garage was closed on 16th September 2011, and the site has since been redeveloped. Routes operated at April 1983 were 5, 15, 23, 101 and 147.

The frontage at Upton Park on Redclyffe Road in 1937. STL 479 is on the left with LT 209 on the right. Some of the stock of ex Independent TD Leylands can be seen inside. (LTM)

An impressive line-up inside the garage in this view taken on 7th August 1936. The buses are STLs 267 and 335, LTs 650, 635, 789, 209, 423, 826 and 906 followed by some of the TD class. Up to the early 1950s, buses here had their fleet numbers painted on the rear dome to assist staff in the running shift office, which was situated at roof level. (LTM)

RM 1257 spent nearly 4 years at Upton Park, and is pictured leaving the garage from the Priory Road exit in January 1976. Routemasters worked from this garage for 18 years during the period covered by this book. (Peter Horner)

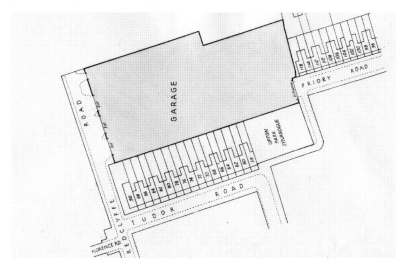

UXBRIDGE (UX)

The garage here opened on 14th June 1922, and was operated on behalf of the LGOC by Thames Valley Traction Co., until the General took over on 1st January 1929. The single shed erected here had an additional one built alongside in 1955, and the two were linked at the rear. In 1937, STs were the double deck allocation, backed up with Dennis Dart and T class single-deckers. Post –war RTs arrived in 1949, and some TD single deck buses came in 1956. New single deck RFs took up duties in 1958. The single deck routes were double decked in 1963, although the RF did return in 1971. RMs came for the 207 in 1963, and later in 1967 the RML, which was later replaced by DMs in 1976. RMs and RMLs later returned in 1980 and 1985. 1971 saw the SMS class arrive and in 1973 the DMS came and the RTs departed. The last classes to appear were the LS in 1980 and the Metrobus in 1981. The garage closed on 2nd December 1983, with work going to a new garage built near the station. Commercial buildings now occupy the site. Routes operated at April 1983 were 98, 128, 204, 207, 222, 223 and 224.

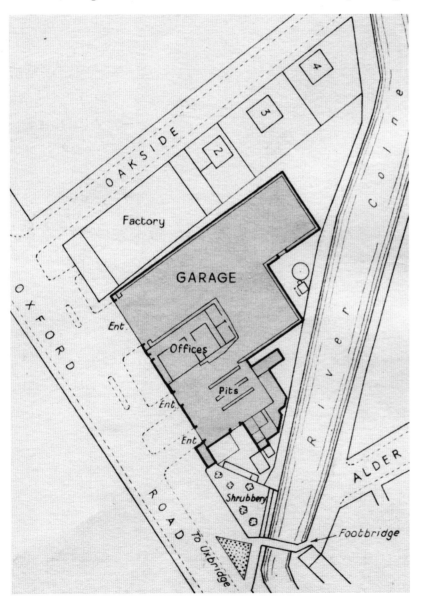

Uxbridge garage in June 1955. The new shed on the left has just been opened and much needed new space provided. The garage was actually a mile or so outside Uxbridge on the Oxford Road in Buckinghamshire. RT 3998 only spent four months at Uxbridge, and it can be seen in this view on the left. (LTM)

The original shed at Uxbridge on its last day, 2nd December 1983. RM 1616 has come in on the 207 and is parked in the doorway. The building is looking very untidy at this point with paint peeling on the doors, and it is clear that no more money was being spent before closure. (Peter Horner)

It is 9pm on 13th November 1967, and RTs 3058 and 1816 are at rest in the new shed at Uxbridge. No Central Area bus routes passed the garage, which was surrounded by LT's country routes. (Mick Webber)

VICTORIA, GILLINGHAM STREET (GM)

The land at Victoria used for the new garage, was already owned by the LGOC, and inherited by London Transport. The new garage was opened on 20th March 1940 with a fleet of 85 STLs. It was unique among LT garages in that it had a basement capable of housing 70 single deck vehicles. The ground floor was designed to accommodate 100 buses. The basement was used in post-war years to house BEA coaches, and also other BTC company vehicles on layover in London. The coaches were generally from Scottish operators and were sometimes to be seen on the ground floor also. RFW coaches were also kept in Victoria basement for a period. RTL 3, with the reversed staircase for showing to potential overseas buyers, was to be found stored in the main garage for a time. All three types of the STD class were operated from here, and some "pre-war" RTs. After the war in 1945, a few Guy Arabs were sent here, but their stay was short. SRTs came in 1949 very briefly, to be replaced by RTs which were superseded by RTLs in 1959, and RMs in 1964. For a short time in May 1950, the garage was part of the experiment to operate RTWs on central London routes. The 8 feet wide buses were banned at the time from working in central London by the police and the working of selected routes for a brief spell was designed to prove them wrong. The 52 was the route in GMs case, and the successful experiment lasted just one week. RTLs left in 1966, and the DMS came between 1972 and 1977. The first Red Arrow routes worked from Gillingham Street in 1966 with XMS class, which was duly replaced by the MBA in 1968, and the SMS in 1979. The LS took over in 1981. A Green Line coach was kept here for a number of years as a standby for breakdowns. The garage closed on 16th July 1993 and the site is now occupied by luxury flats. Routes operated at April 1983 were 2B, 52A, 500, 507 and Round London tours.

Above right: A view of Gillingham Street garage showing two buses ready for Red Arrow service, and a double deck Standerwick coach taking a break before heading back north from the coach station. The exit from the basement for single deck vehicles, is via a ramp on the corner of Guildhouse Street on the far right, with the entrance inside the garage via a ramp on the left hand side. (Gerald Mead)

Right: A typical night scene at a London bus garage. RM 2047 has had its rear blind removed, and waits by the far left hand door. The Routemaster had a constant presence here from 1964 until closure. Some of the Red Arrow fleet can be seen in the background. (Terry Cooper Collection/Mick Webber)

Wartime in Gillingham Street. The buses all carry their head lamp masks and white mudguard paint in this scene which shows STLs 2081, 1997, 2161 and 2395, beyond which there are three LTs and more STLs. It is 12th June 1940, and the garage had been open nearly three months. (LTM)

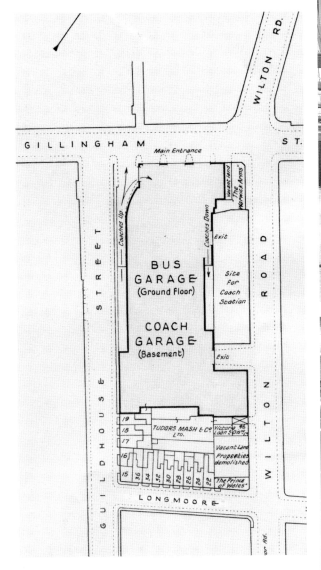

RM 826 spent five years at Gillingham Street, and has just returned from a duty on route 137 showing the run in blind "Chelsea Bridge Road". (Peter Horner)

WALTHAMSTOW (WW)

Walthamstow Urban District Council built their tram depot here opening in 1905. London Transport converted it to trolleybus operation in October 1936, and this remained the case until 1960, when buses replaced trolleybuses in two stages, finishing in April. New Routemasters took over until they were joined by RTs between 1964 and 1977. RMLs were allocated from 1966 to 1968. New MB and MBS classes came with the new Victoria line, and the local reshaping plan in 1968. The DMSs first worked here in 1974, and the RMs departed in 1981 when the garage became all one man operated, and the Titan took over. It closed on 23rd November 1991, and although the garage has been demolished, the Municipal Offices building remains but the rest of the site is now occupied by housing. Routes operated at April 1983 were 34, 97, 97A, 123, 144, 158, 212, 255 and 275.

The ornate Edwardian Municipal Tramway Office is a listed building, and happily survives today. RM 148 pulls out into Chingford Road on route 58, the original replacement of trolleybus route 685. It displays the plain London Transport gold fleet name without the underlining. It is May 1973. (Peter Horner)

DMSs 1850 and 1839 were delivered new to Walthamstow in June 1975, and are blinded up for the circular route W21. The garage has not changed much from trolleybus days, and the bricked up section on the left is the former tower wagon shed. Many trams were scrapped here before the war on waste land just behind the depot on the far right. (Capital Transport)

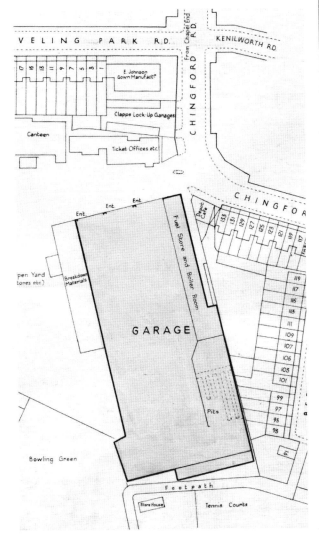

A 1977 view inside Walthamstow garage showing RTs 4166, 1152, and 502 with RM 1222. Twelve RTs were needed for route 34, although that was to change to DMS later that year. (Peter Horner)

WALWORTH (WL)

The horse tram depot here opened in 1871, and was converted to electric power in 1903. It was known as Camberwell depot until 1950, when it was renamed Walworth to avoid confusion with Camberwell bus garage which was just across the other side of Camberwell New Road. Trams were swept away from here in 1950/51, and a batch of 50 RTLs arrived. The new rebuilt garage was not complete at this stage, and buses had to be serviced at Camberwell (Q) until the final work was finished in 1954. The RTW class came in 1958, and they were replaced by the RM in 1965,

the RTLs being superseded by RTs in 1966. The Red Arrow MBAs came in 1968 and stayed until the LS took over in 1981. RTs left in 1976. The DMS class worked here between 1971 and 1982 with DMs, and the Titan arrived in 1982. The garage closed on 1st November 1985 and most work went to Camberwell. It has since reopened and closed several times, and at the time of writing remains in use. Routes operated at April 1983 were 12, 45, 176, 184, 185 and 501.

A late 1970s view at Walworth. DMSs 62 and 15 are parked out of service from the 185, whilst New Cross RM 1441 makes its way out on to the 171. The canteen block here is on the right of this view. (Terry Cooper Collection/Mick Webber)

MBAs 600, 537 and 541, seen on 2nd May 1981, are all in from working Red Arrow route 501. Fifteen vehicles were needed to work this Mon-Fri route. (Peter Horner)

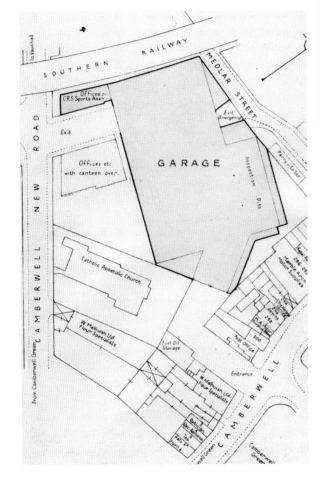

The garage offices are on the left in this early 1960s scene at Walworth. Highgate RM 595 waits on the 17, with RTL 1622 behind and RTW 6 on the right. The 17 replaced trolleybus route 517/617 in 1961, and was extended south to Camberwell Green. (Mick Webber)

WANDSWORTH (WD)

Opened as a horse tram depot in 1883, it was extensively rebuilt and converted to electric-conduit operation by the LCC in 1906. London Transport partially converted it to trolleybus operation in 1937, and both trams and trolleybuses worked side by side until both were withdrawn in September 1950. Seventy five new RTs arrived to take over the new routes, but were replaced by RTLs after a few months. The RTs, however, returned in 1967 to replace the RTLs. The RM first came in 1970, and when DMs were allocated in 1975, the RTs finally departed. In 1980, the RMs took over from the DM. DMSs came in 1971, being replaced by the Metrobus in 1983. The garage closed on 11th July 1987, although it was reopened as a home for London Coaches and the Round London Sightseeing Tour in April 1988. Routes operated at April 1983 were 28, 44, 220, 295, N68 and N88.

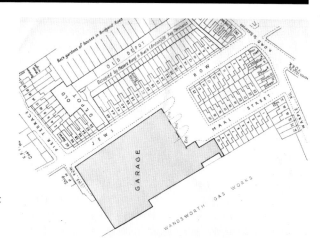

A view of Wandsworth garage taken in May 1971 when the RT dominated. The houses between Marl Street and Jews Row have just been demolished revealing the modernised front with the original tram sheds behind. (Peter Horner)

New RTs arrived at Wandsworth in September 1950 to replace both trams and trolleybuses, but they were soon replaced by RTLs after only a few months. This scene shows the pit area with RTLs 1171, 1075, 1167 and 1103 in December 1951. The RTL reigned supreme here for the next sixteen years. (LTM)

WEST GREEN (WG)

The garage here was the base for the "Admiral" bus services from 1922, which subsequently passed to the London Public, and then the LGOC in 1929. In the London Transport era, it was the last garage to operate the NS class in 1937. ST and T class single deckers shared the allocation during that year. After the war, RTLs came in 1949 and were the main class throughout until closure, although some RTWs appeared between 1949 and 1951. Single deck Qs and later RFs were also allocated.
In 1961 new RMs 753-757 arrived to work a share of the 269 as part of the trolleybus conversion scheme. The garage closed on 2nd January 1962, and in the reshuffle of buses at the time, West Green RTLs went to West Ham just before this date, and some RTs went in the other direction giving WG an RT allocation for just a few days before closure. Work was transferred to Wood Green, Palmers Green and Tottenham. Maximum vehicle requirement operated at time of closure was 66 and routes operated were 29, 29a, 144, 217, 231, 233 and 269. Part of the site is now occupied by housing.

A 1959 view of West Green garage with Metro Cammell bodied RTL 842 leaving for route 144. The building looks more like industrial units than s bus garage without any signage to denote its use or ownership. (LTM)

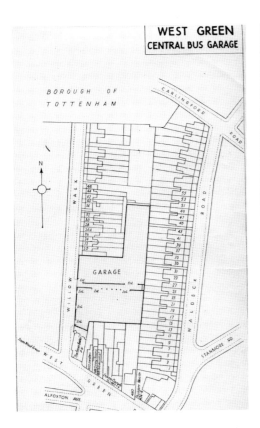

WEST GREEN
CENTRAL BUS GARAGE

The garage at West Green was cramped, and certainly would have been no use for bigger more modern buses. RTL 842 is nearest the camera whilst RTL 1353 is parked in the dead end section, with the stairs to the offices on the right of centre. (LTM)

WEST HAM (WH)

West Ham Corporation Tramways first worked from here in 1906, and that form of transport continued here until London Transport replaced the trams with trolleybuses from 1937. An overhaul facility for the trolleybuses existed here. Buses took over in stages, finishing in 1960, when new Routemasters took over along with RTs from Forest Gate, which closed at the same time. The RTs were replaced by RTLs between 1962 and 1968, when they returned until 1972. Some RMLs were used between 1966 and 1972, and again from 1976 to 1982. New MBSs were here between 1969 and 1975 and DMSs from 1971 to 1982. Later the SMS and DM classes arrived, and in 1982 the Titan started to gradually take over. The garage was closed on 10th October 1992. Routes operated at April 1983 were 5, 25, 58, 69, 86, 173, 225, 241, 262, 278, S1 and N99. Most of the site is now occupied by housing in Routemaster Close, although the original tramway office block remains.

RTLs 223 and 1587 feature in this scene taken on 12th March 1967. The pit area building is in the centre with the main shed behind. An overhauling workshop existed beyond the pit area in tram and trolleybus days. (Mick Webber)

RM I was used as a training vehicle from 1959, and was used extensively in east London until withdrawn in 1972. Much of that time it was allocated to West Ham, and it is parked here in the late 1960s with one of the two Austin towing lorries delivered in 1957 to the right. (Alan Cross)

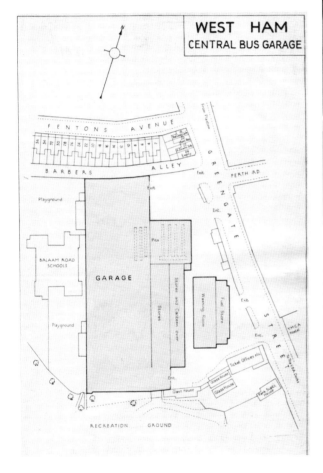

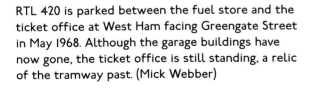

RTL 420 is parked between the fuel store and the ticket office at West Ham facing Greengate Street in May 1968. Although the garage buildings have now gone, the ticket office is still standing, a relic of the tramway past. (Mick Webber)

WESTBOURNE PARK (X)

This most unusual garage was opened on 15th August 1981, and replaced garages at Stonebridge Park and Middle Row which closed the night before. It inherited the code "X" from Middle Row. It is built between a canal and railway, and has the elevated A40 running across its roof. The building can accommodate up to 110 buses, and was supplied with 78 when opened with RMs and DMs. Routes operated at April 1983 were 7, 18, 28 and 31.

Surely the most unusual of all bus garages in London, Westbourne Park is built underneath the A40 with an entrance on Great Western Road. RM 22 is central to this view taken in the first months of operation. (LTM)

RMs 259 and 939 inside Westbourne Park in August 1981. Both of these buses had come from Middle Row. The floor of the garage has yet to accumulate dirt and oil stains. (Peter Horner)

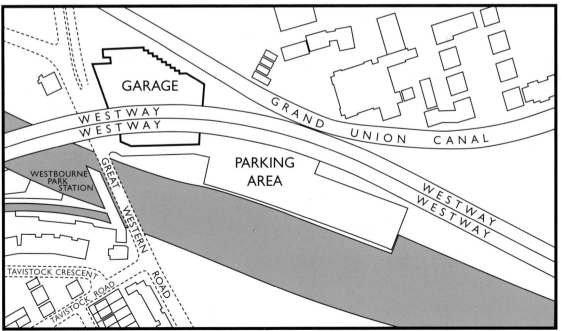

WILLESDEN (AC)

The LGOC garage here was opened on 7th October 1912. In the 1930s ST and STL types were the main allocation. In post-war years the RT first came on the scene in 1949, with the RTW in 1951. RTLs replaced the RTs in 1955, but the RT returned after the RTLs left in 1968. This was the last garage to operate the RTL in passenger service in November 1968. One of the Routemaster prototypes, RML 3, first worked here on route 8 in 1959. The RTWs left and were replaced by RMs in 1965 and RMLs came in 1966. The RT survived here until 1976. SMS class buses came in 1970 and the DMS arrived in 1978 being superseded by the Metrobus in 1980. The garage remains open. Routes operated at April 1983 were 6, 52, 226, 260, 297 and N91.

The door to Willesden garage between Churchmead Road and Bertie Road in the late 1930s. A monument to the war dead can be seen to the right of the door, and this aspect of the garage remains unchanged. (LTM)

In 1965 route I was operated by New Cross and Catford during Mon-Fri and New Cross on Sunday, but on Saturday Willesden supplied RTWs for a short period to work alongside the New Cross RTs. RTW 8 arrived at Willesden after overhaul in April 1962, and remained until it was transferred to Brixton in September 1965. It is seen here in the yard at its home garage, having terminated there before its journey back to south London. (Capital Transport)

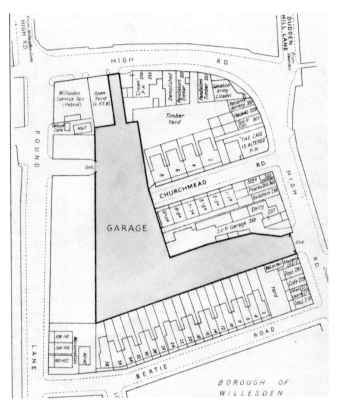

The doorway to the garage in the High Road between Churchmead Road, and Pound Lane. RTL 1151 has worked the 52A, which was a weekday route that terminated on the forecourt of Colindale trolleybus depot. The depot closed on 3rd January 1962, and the route was withdrawn. (Terry Cooper Collection/Mick Webber)

Overleaf: A wonderful view inside Willesden on 23rd August 1936. On the left is STL 36, and on the far right we can see STL 330, with ST 339 in the centre. Behind ST 339 are STL 4, C 95, STL 309, ST 715 and a double deck Q. The Q is either Q 2 or Q 3, as both were allocated to Middle Row at this time for route 52. Perhaps it was in for maintenance. (LTM)

WOOD GREEN (WN)

The North Metropolitan built their horse tram depot on this site in 1895, and in 1905, the Metropolitan Electric Tramways converted it to electric tramway operation. London Transport subsequently changed over to trolleybuses here in 1938. The original building had a forecourt, but the depot was later extended to cover this area. The trolleybuses were replaced by buses in two stages, ending in November 1961, after a short period where both buses and trolleybuses worked together. New Routemasters took over, and they were joined by some RTs in January 1962 when nearby West Green garage closed. New flat fare routes brought the MBS class to Wood Green in 1968, and some RMLs were used in 1970/71. The DMS first made an appearance in 1973 with the RTs and the MBSs leaving in 1974. The DM class came in 1975, but in 1981, Metrobuses started to arrive, and they would replace the DMS and DMs by 1982. The garage remains in operation. Routes operated at April 1983 were 29, 41, 84A, 141, 221, W2, W3 and N29.

Wood Green garage from the High Road in the mid-1960s. The internal dividing wall in the centre of the picture marks the original end of the building, the area forward of that being the extension over the old forecourt. (Mick Webber)

Transition period at Wood Green. Between April and November 1961, the garage operated both buses and trolleybuses. An unidentified Routemaster is in the pit area minus its grille, whilst K1 class trolleybus 1297 on the left, waits for work. An Albion breakdown tender is parked between them. (Terry Cooper Collection/ Mick Webber)

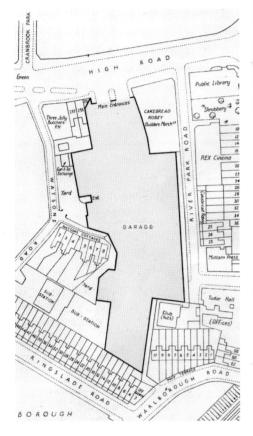

RT 39 is a trainer and stands next to RM 600 which carries blinds for the trolleybus replacement route 269; it entered service new here in April 1961. The traverser pit and turntable can be seen in the foreground, and trolleybus presence remains in the background. (Terry Cooper Collection/Mick Webber)

TOTALS OF BUSES SCHEDULED FOR SERVICE 1933 AND 1983

July 1933

Garage	M-F	Sat	Sun	Garage	M-F	Sat	Sun
A	60	62	54	N	73	69	64
AB	49	49	45	P	84	83	72
AC	123	122	98	PB	48	49	48
AD	79	74	68	Q	138	130	101
AE	100	95	74	R	93	90	89
AF	80	82	55	RD	40	39	40
AH	95	92	91	S	40	36	36
AK	70	59	57	SP	54	56	48
AL	189	186	174	T	180	176	164
AM	69	72	53	TB	80	80	85
AP	76	77	76	TC	80	79	87
AR	143	143	101	TL	137	139	147
AV	65	71	55	U	159	154	151
B	89	90	57	UX	13	13	6
BK	89	86	68	V	86	89	65
C	70	70	54	W	142	135	102
CF	103	92	83	WG	64	64	51
CL	46	45	45	X	85	78	71
D	128	124	108				
E	88	89	71				
ED	91	97	63				
EW	23	23	23				
F	86	84	71				
G	100	93	82				
H	58	57	43				
HD	53	54	49				
HW	100	101	95				
J	164	150	129				
K	29	34	34				
L	27	23	26				
M	84	77	61				
MH	48	49	42				

April 1983

Garage	M-F	Sat	Sun	Garage	M-F	Sat	Sun
A	58	52	18	M	23	20	12
AC	57	51	28	MH	50	44	23
AD	52	37	18	NB	51	50	22
AE	39	35	14	NS	75	71	20
AF	60	40	26	NX	123	77	46
AG	115	66	46	ON	62	58	24
AK	54	44	26	PB	31	26	11
AL	119	96	41	PD	86	75	34
AP	54	43	19	PM	125	94	45
AR	100	69	40	PR	56	45	23
AV	68	61	31	Q	79	47	34
B	25	23	10	R	32	28	13
BK	87	80	26	RD	44	44	11
BN	67	38	20	S	44	36	15
BW	78	56	38	SF	53	36	25
BX	59	56	22	SP	70	46	26
CA	50	40	17	SW	76	42	30
CF	59	28	17	T	59	44	22
CT	40	38	21	TB	79	69	26
E	65	46	24	TC	102	83	32
ED	64	46	22	TH	72	46	20
EM	58	50	22	TL	157	117	49
EW	52	46	16	U	84	64	32
FW	76	70	34	UX	52	47	22
FY	55	43	18	V	54	51	37
GM	37	24	13	W	87	79	38
HD	59	45	19	WD	45	32	17
HL	64	61	26	WH	116	83	43
HT	126	99	71	WL	65	43	23
HW	75	66	34	WN	73	59	27
K	35	27	16	WW	80	66	36
L	32	30	14	X	62	46	28